WINE MAKING
THE NATURAL WAY

D1440020

WINE MAKING
THE NATURAL WAY

by

IAN BALL

PAPERFRONTS
ELLIOT RIGHT WAY BOOKS
KINGSWOOD, SURREY, U.K.

CONTENTS

Chapter		Page
	Introduction	7
1	Good Health	11
2	What makes country wine?	17
3	Equipment	21
4	Safety and cleanliness	29
5	Sterilising equipment	31
6	Storage	32
7	Collecting ingredients	36
8	Plants best avoided	39
9	Preserving ingredients	40
10	Wine records	42
11	Chemical-free wines	46
12	Sugar-free wines	49
13	Honey in wine	51
14	Starting a fermentation	53
15	Racking	61
16	Clearing	64
17	Bottling	66
18	Smarten your bottles	69
19	Serving wine	71
20	Vinegar	74
21	Useful things to make	76
22	What goes wrong with wine	80
23	Sparkling wine	83
24	Liqueurs	86
25	Notes on recipes	89
26	Quick index	91
27	Recipes for cheats:	92

Pure apple juice   Pure grapefruit juice
Pure blackcurrant juice   Pure orange juice
Pure apple & blackcurrant   Pure pineapple juice
  juice

28 Wine planner   105
29 Recipes – country wines   107

Agrimony	Hawthorn blossom
Apple	Hop
Apricot	Mead
Barley	Nettle
Beetroot	Oak Leaf
Blackberry	Parsley
Blackcurrant	Parsnip
Carrot	Peach
Celery	Peppermint
Cherry	Plum
Christmas Punch	Raspberry
Coltsfoot	Rice and raisin
Dandelion	Rose Petal
Elderberry	Rosehip
Elderflower	Sloe
Ginger	Strawberry
Gooseberry	Tea and Prune

Introduction

A lot of complicated nonsense is written and spoken about wine making. Natural, nourishing country wines are simple to make.

'All the best things in life are free,' runs the wise old saying and quality wines, made the natural way, need cost only a few pence per bottle – if you know how.

This book shows you, in easy to follow step-by-step instructions, exactly how to produce your own superb wines, most of them ready for drinking after a few months.

These days everything new in the food line seems to be dehydrated or frozen and chock-a-block with chemicals.

Flavourless, watery wine is sold by supermarkets.

Country wine is made from wholesome natural ingredients – flowers, fruit, grain, herbs and vegetables. They are free for gathering, packed with vitamins, nutritious and good for us.

Wine was made by our ancestors a few generations ago for enjoyment and health and cost them next to nothing.

You do not need much equipment to make traditional country wines. My grandmother made wine at home without lots of paraphernalia.

Recipes in this book take full advantage of the health-giving properties of natural ingredients, which pass on their goodness in the finished wine.

Should you prefer not to put sugar (sucrose) or chemicals in your country wines, there are clear instructions for making wine with recipes using only the natural sugar (fructose and glucose) found in fruit and honey and *without adding chemicals*.

If you live in a city or town – most of us do – do not be put off by references to 'country' recipes, because ingredients are readily accessible to the town dweller.

Home wine making is not a new idea. From the beginning

of written history we read of peoples of every nation making their own distinctive liquors from freely available fruit, grain, flowers, herbs, vegetables and trees.

Each family made wine for its own consumption and if there was any to spare, friends were welcome to join them in enjoying the surplus.

Wine making was a well established country craft long before the industrial revolution lured people away from villages into industrialised towns, where many traditional country recipes, knowledge and skills were lost and forgotten.

Today, old recipes are difficult to find and unless we guard them, they will disappear.

In this book I set out to recapture the sense of well-being and self-sufficiency long associated with country wine making that we are in danger of losing.

It is ironic that the present huge revival of this relaxing pleasant, satisfying and rewarding pastime has been stimulated by equipment sales which make it appear an unnecessarily expensive and overly – technical business.

Beware! What started as a simple rustic craft, easily understood and enjoyed by everyone, is increasingly becoming an artificially complicated ritual with its own mysterious language and 'specialist' equipment. Rest assured, the craft can still be easy to learn, inexpensive and all of us can relax and enjoy it, particularly the end product.

Making your own wine is fun!

Just consider some advantages of making wine. For a few pence you can start building a cellar of wines, offering a wide choice of bottles to improve every social occasion. Your meals can be cooked with wine and accompanied by a bottle of Chateau Excellent Whatever You Like. The variety of country wines is large and there is one to complement every menu.

As well as enjoying new and exotic dishes you can hold frequent parties without worrying about the ever increasing cost of buying commercial wine. Should you prefer your own company, a quiet evening at home takes on a fresh, pleasurable dimension. You will be surprised at the number of people calling to see you once they know a bottle of wine is likely to be opened.

Bottles of wine make a perfect gift.

Do not worry about having insufficient room for making and storing wine. Whether you live in a bed-sit, or a house, there is ALWAYS somewhere.

NOTE:

To help you find everything you need to know about making country wine, an easy-to-use, quick index to principles and methods is given on page 91.

With this you can instantly locate the information you want.

1

Good Health!

Medically, it is fairly well established that, in the western world, stress is a major contributory cause of death.

Wine taken in moderation, relaxes and invigorates. It helps us to unwind and see pressures and worries in their true perspective and it sharpens our senses.

Drinking a sensible amount of wine regularly is conducive to our good health and longevity.

For the maker of natural country wines there are two bonuses: firstly, the nutritional value of ingredients is not lost in the wine making process and secondly, the medicinal qualities traditionally associated with fruit, flowers, herbs, vegetables and grain are retained in the wine; this beneficial aspect of country winemaking should not be overlooked.

Today, nutrients and medicines are often chemically reproduced and mass marketed but lots are freely available to us in their natural form in the countryside. Many of the modern medicines prescribed to us by doctors for common ailments are derived principally from flowers, fruit, vegetables and herbs.

Although now unfamiliar to most of us, the recipes for a number of these remedies were known to country folk one or more generations ago. Natural ingredients became carefully chosen because experience over dozens of lifetimes had shown them to have special properties.

Over the past twenty years, orthodox medical theory has been substantially revised and the dismissive attitude towards ancient remedies has in many instances been replaced by an admission that healing properties once popularly attributed to particular plants often do have a basis in fact.

Orthodox medical theory tends to rest on the principle

that there may be one or more identifiable active ingredients in some plants which can be isolated and offered as medicine. However, it is increasingly recognised that these identifiable active ingredients in the plants may be accompanied by previously unidentified, passive elements, which correct imbalance and improve beneficial effect without the undesirable and dangerous side-effects of some modern medicines.

This being the case, it is desirable to use the plant in as close to its original form as possible. The wine making process draws much goodness from the plant used and offers it in the finished wine.

Bearing in mind the medicinal qualities traditionally associated with particular plants, here is a list, by no means exhaustive, of flowers, vegetables, herbs, grain and fruit, used in country wine making, together with the curative properties commonly credited to them.

Wines made from these ingredients taste excellent and, if taken in moderation they can help heal, are doubly excellent.

The recipes are in this book.

This list is included for your interest and information only. No claims are made for the healing qualities of these wines and you must realize that the traditional medicinal value of ingredients is, in many cases, not yet medically proven.

If you are ill, see your doctor. Never presume that a glass or two of wine can be a panacea or cure-all.

Ask him also whether it is safe for you to drink wine while taking any medication he might prescribe.

Selection of curative properties traditionally and popularly credited to natural ingredients used in country wines:
Agrimony: Tonic. Strengthens and tones muscles. Eases coughs. Purifies the blood. Helps kidneys –diuretic.
Apple: Rich in vitamins and minerals. Extremely beneficial to general health and well-being. Improves skin complexion and clears up skin disorders. Assists digestion. Eases catarrh, asthma and breathing problems. Fortifies blood

and lessens effects of arthritis.

Apricot: High in iron and minerals. Strengthens blood and combats anaemia. Helps cure bronchitis; loosens catarrh. Clears constipation.

Barley: Ancient food. Rich source of vitamins and protein. Highly nutritious. Easily digested by the sick and the convalescent. Relieves asthma and prevents loss of hair.

Beetroot: Fortifies blood. Helps cure skin disorders. Eases headaches and reduces inflammation of the kidneys and bladder. Clears constipation. Reduces nervous complaints and menstruation problems.

Blackberry: General tonic and blood purifier. Helps clear up skin disorders. Beneficial to sufferers of arthritis, rheumatism and anaemia. Remedy for constipation and diarrhoea.

Blackcurrant: Rich in vitamins. Highly nutritious. Natural antiseptic – soothes and assists healing of sore throats. Purifies blood and helps in cases of anaemia.

Carrot: Rich in vitamin A. Commonly believed to improve eyesight and used in folk medicine to cure cataracts, night-blindness and other eye troubles. Improves skin complexion and reduces any build-up of fluid in body tissue. Also beneficial in cases of asthma, catarrh, high blood pressure, colitis and constipation.

Celery: Remedy for arthritis, rheumatism, asthma, catarrh and high blood pressure. Reduces accumulation of fluid in body tissue.

Cherry: Helps cure anaemia and poor skin complexion. Eases arthritis, rheumatism and gout. Relieves catarrh, constipation and high blood pressure.

Coltsfoot: Rich in vitamin C. Eases catarrh, coughing, and chest complaints. Its Latin name means cough.

Dandelion: General tonic and blood purifier. Eases rheumatism. Beneficial in cases of anaemia, poor circulation and low blood pressure. Reduces accumulation of fluid in body tissue. Laxative and diuretic.

Elderberry: Tonic and blood purifier. Cure for sore throats, bronchitis, asthma, coughs, colds, catarrh; and constipation.

Elderflower: Remedy for jaundice, sore throats, colds and

digestive upsets. Sleep inducing.

Ginger: Stimulant. Cure for colds and indigestion.

Gooseberry: Remedy for arthritis, catarrh, poor complexion, constipation and indigestion.

Grape: Highly nutritious. Blood purifier. Remedy for anaemia and skin disorders, asthma, sore throats, catarrh and constipation.

Grapefruit: Benefits skin complexion and aids digestion. Natural antiseptic – cures colds and relieves arthritis.

Hawthorn Blossom: Strengthens heart muscles. Improves breathing.

Honey: Rich in nutrients and mineral salts. Rejuvenating. Soothes nerves and strengthens heart muscle. Remedy for anaemia, arthritis and rheumatism. Used as an aphrodisiac from the earliest times.

Hop: Purifies the blood. Relieves headaches and stomach complaints. Sleep inducing.

Lemon: Rich in vitamin C. Tonic. Natural antiseptic. Cure for colds and influenza. Clears up skin disorders. Beneficial effect on headaches and coughs. Eases asthma.

Nettle: Purifies blood. General tonic, rejuvenating. Rich in vitamin C – guards against colds and influenza. Beneficial in cases of asthma, rheumatism and gout.

Orange: Remedy for asthma, bronchitis, high blood pressure and rheumatism.

Parsley: Rich in vitamins, iron and minerals. Remedy for anaemia, arthritis, menstruation disorders and high blood pressure. Relieves indigestion and reduces accumulation of fluid in body tissue.

Parsnip: Remedy for gout and colitis. Diuretic.

Peach: Rich in vitamins and minerals. Improves skin complexion and is beneficial in treatment of anaemia, asthma, high blood pressure, constipation and digestion.

Peppermint: Refreshing and invigorating. Relieves indigestion, colds, headaches, nausea, stomach-ache and diarrhoea.

Pineapple: High in vitamins and minerals. Assists digestion. Remedy for arthritis, catarrh, high blood pressure and constipation.

Plum: Invigorating and rejuvenating. Clears up skin

disorders. Relieves sore throats and bronchitis. Eases digestion. Laxative.

Prunes: Dried plums. See above.

Raisins: Dried black grapes. See grape.

Raspberry: Eases high blood pressure, menstrual pain and constipation.

Rice: Rich in vitamins and minerals. Remedy for diarrhoea.

Rosehip: Rich in vitamin C. Helps guard against colds, influenza and other bodily infections.

Strawberry: Purifies the blood. Clears up skin disorders. Remedy for rheumatism, high blood pressure and constipation.

Sultanas: Dried white grapes. See grape.

REMEMBER the warning given at the beginning of this list, on page 12. In addition it must be emphasised that seeking a cure by drinking large quantities of country wine may worsen your condition and could lead to alcoholism and related physical and mental disorders.

2
What Makes Country Wine?

Country wine is the end product of a chemical reaction between a composition of elements in a process called fermentation, during which wine yeast acts on natural sugar (fructose and glucose) present principally in fruit and honey, or a combination of natural sugar and processed household sugar (sucrose) to form alcohol.

After fermentation has ceased the wine continues developing in a complicated way as it matures and the result is a smooth, pleasant and satisfying beverage, which can accompany and complement food or be enjoyed by itself.

Country wine is made up of a number of constituent parts:

1. Acid
2. Flavour
3. Natural sugar (fructose and glucose); or some natural sugar (fructose and glucose) plus household sugar (sucrose)
4. Nutrient
5. Tannin
6. Water
7. Wine yeast
8. Alcohol

Together, these elements form the body of a wine. Let us examine the contribution each part makes in the development of country wine.

Acid

Fruits have their own particular types of acid. Vegetables, grain, flowers, herbs and leaves have almost none.

Most country wines require the addition of acid.

Acid is the foundation of a good wine and in the early stages of fermentation it inhibits development of hostile bacteria and encourages the activity of wine yeast. It influences for the better the flavour and development of wine and helps it keep. Acid mellows with age, becoming less obvious in wine as it matures.

Too much acid makes wine tart or sour. Too little leaves it lifeless and insipid.

By following the recipes you avoid problems.

Recipes in this book use natural citric acid in juice extracted from oranges and lemons. This is a wholesome, nutritious way of adding acid to your wine.

Flavour

The main ingredient decides the flavour and colour of your finished wine. The rough taste at the start bears no resemblance to the smooth, succulent and appetizing flavour of the mature wine.

Natural sugar (fructose and glucose) and household sugar (sucrose)

Multiplying wine yeast feeds on natural sugar (fructose and glucose) and household sugar (sucrose) in a process called fermentation. Alcohol is a by-product of the wine yeast's breeding.

The amount of natural sugar (fructose and glucose) and household sugar (sucrose) eaten up by the wine yeast during fermentation decides the level of alcohol in your wine. This remains fixed and is not affected by the length of time your wine is stored.

Originally, country wines relied exclusively on natural sugar (fructose and glucose) found in honey and fruit to ferment alcohol. Honey and a measure of fruit were included, in varying degrees, in most country recipes.

Today, few of us have free access to fruit and honey, and the cheapest way of producing alcohol is to supplement the natural sugar (fructose and glucose) content of ingredients with processed cane and beet sugar (sucrose) in the form of granulated household sugar.

However, if you are prepared to pay not so very much more per bottle of wine, you can choose to make your superb natural wines in true country style by using honey and grape juice in place of household sugar (sucrose).

Should you decide to use household sugar (sucrose), ordinary granulated sugar is best. Demerara sugar lends a distinctive taste and golden colour to wine and may be used in recipes where a heavy body is required.

Nutrient

Wine yeast requires nutrient for nourishment while working to produce alcohol. Some ingredients possess a poor balance of nutrients, and recipes in this book use small quantities of raisins (dried black grapes) or sultanas (dried white grapes), rich in vitamins, to compensate for deficiencies.

A ¼ *tea*spoon of yeast extract, Marmite or pure malt extract, is added to get the wine yeast off to a strong and rapid start.

Tannin

Tannin is present in the skins of many fruits, including apples, blackcurrants, elderberries, grapes, plums and sloes. It is also present in oak leaves. Grain, vegetables, flowers and herbs have little or no tannin and it is desirable to add some to most wines.

Tannin lends bite and tang to flavour and protects wine from bacteria and possible ill-effects from over-exposure to air. It helps clear the finished wine.

When insufficient tannin is included in a recipe the wine tastes flat and lacks character. In excess it tastes rough and harsh.

Tannin mellows with age.

Tea is a rich natural source of tannin and tea brewed from loose leaves or bags may be used. Dregs from a recently brewed pot are usable.

Water

It does not matter whether water is hard or soft, chlorinated or unchlorinated.

Cold water carries air which is used by wine yeast in the initial stage of fermentation.

Wine yeast

Wine yeast (saccharomyces ellipsoideus) is a living organism, a plant; classified as a single-celled fungus. It lives, feeds and breeds on sugary substances and a by-product of its multiplying is alcohol.

Wine yeast remains inactive in extremely cold conditions, lying dormant until things warm up before resuming activity. It functions most efficiently at a temperature of 18°C (64°F). Wine yeast is resistant to temperatures of up to about 38°C (100°F). It cannot survive above 49°C (120°F).

Buy wine yeast either as dry granules or tablets to be reactivated in water, or as a pure, natural culture, living in a liquid or jelly medium in a phial.

An all-purpose wine yeast is suitable for country wines but you can experiment with special wine yeast strains like Chablis, Champagne, Hock and Mead for white wines and Bordeaux, Burgundy, Port and Sherry for red wines.

Most recipes in this book produce table wines slightly above standard commercial wine strength, fermenting to about 12% alcohol per volume (21% proof). Wine yeast ferments stronger wines if more sugar is added, either natural sugar (fructose and glucose) in the form of grape juice and honey or processed household sugar (sucrose).

An alcohol concentration of 17% alcohol per volume (30% proof) is possible. However, after your wine has achieved an alcohol level of 17% alcohol per volume (30% proof) wine yeast is normally inhibited from further activity.

Each recipe gives an indication of the level of alcohol likely to be reached.

Alcohol

The central and essential part of wine.

Ethyl alcohol is the main alcohol created in wine and other beverages by wine yeast's fermentation of natural sugar (fructose and glucose) or household sugar (sucrose).

Alcohol is often used for medicinal purposes and its therapeutic and beneficial qualities are well documented. Taken regularly and in moderation, it is not harmful and for centuries has played an important part in folk medicine. The very real dangers of drinking it to excess are equally well documented and need hardly be expanded upon here but be warned.

3
Equipment

There is no need to dash out and buy equipment. First, see what you already have.

Then visit your local home brew stockist to view the wide range of articles on sale.

Much equipment, though adding to the cost of making wine, may save you time and effort and the friendly, knowledgeable staff are always pleased to offer helpful advice.

Here is a list of marketed items, together with practical, money saving alternatives. You need:

Bucket or bin
A plastic bucket, or bin, or wide-mouthed vessel of at least 2 gallons (9 litres), preferably 4 gallons (18 litres), capacity. Be certain it is non-toxic and suitable for food use. If you are unsure, be safe and buy a bucket or bin sold for wine making and brewing.

The container is for fermenting natural ingredients like flowers, fruit, herbs, vegetables and grain during the first stage of wine making and should be wide-mouthed to make it easy for you to add all ingredients and stir regularly.

Fermentation vessels
For the second stage of wine making, where fermenting wine is strained, the solids are thrown away and fermentation continued with wine only, you need two or three 1 gallon (4½ litres) fermentation vessels.

In shops you are invited to buy 1 gallon (4½ litres) narrow-necked glass jars, called demijohns. These are excellent for fermenting wine but any *thick* glass or non-toxic plastic, or polythene vessel which has not held a poisonous chemical and has a capacity of approximately 1 gallon (4½ litres) will do.

Getting large, empty spirit bottles for use as fermentation vessels is easy. You have seen them fastened over optics in pubs and clubs. These are ideal, hold a fraction less than 1 gallon (4½ litres) and are thrown out by staff when empty. If you ask nicely, they are happy to give you a few and even save them for you, if they know you will collect regularly. A friend of mine picked up three or four a week and eventually had so many, he started giving them away.

Ask round for large plastic or polythene containers. Shops sometimes have fruit juices delivered in 1 gallon (4½ litres) containers and fill their own bottles with the contents – seek and ye shall find. A phone call often pays dividends.

I knew a winemaker who fermented his wines in a large, transparent plastic bag, supported in a strong cardboard or wooden box.

Should you decide to follow his example make sure the bag is big and strong enough to hold 1 gallon (4½ litres) of liquid and test it for leaks by running in a few pints of cold water to rinse out after you have sterilised it. *Never use coloured bags*. If you are satisfied it is not holed, put the bag in a box and pour in your ingredients. Bunch up the mouth of the bag and tie it with string or an elastic band. Cushion the bag with folded newspaper, if you wish.

Congratulations! You are the proud owner of a collapsible, easily stored fermentation vessel.

Storage vessels
After fermentation has finished you need a suitable vessel for storing your wine to clear and mature before bottling.

Narrow-necked 1 gallon (4½ litres) glass jars, or spirit bottles are ideal. Narrow-necked 1 gallon (4½ litres) non-toxic plastic and polythene vessels may be used for storage, providing the plastic or polythene is at least 2mm thick. Thinner than this, too much air permeates through and spoils your wine.

You need several storage vessels.

Bottles
Each gallon (4½ litres) of wine fills six-and-a-half standard

size wine bottles, so acquire a number of bottles, including a few half-size ones.

Wine bottles are sold by your home brew stockist but finding a free supply is simple. Pubs, clubs, hotels, restaurants and wine bars throw away crates of empty bottles every week. They are usually pleased for you to take as many as you want, if you ask. You are doing them a favour because it makes space in their backyards – for more discarded bottles.

Any sort of bottle may be used, but real wine bottles look best. Cider bottles are acceptable. Hoard Champagne bottles; *they are essential for sparkling wines.*

Never be squeamish when collecting bottles. No matter how mucky the bottle looks or how much mould is festering in the bottom, properly rinsed with hot water and sterilised with sulphite solution (sodium metabisulphite mixed with water, see page 31) not a single germ survives.

If you have the nerve for it and like meeting people, you might follow the example of a friend of mine who recently took an interest in our craft.

He stood in front of the local bottle bank on a Saturday

afternoon and asked each person approaching with a wine bottle in hand, if he could offer the bottle a home in his winery. He collected twenty-six wine bottles in an hour.

It may prove an interesting way of making new friends. After all, you have a liking for wine in common and that is not a bad start.

Never feel you are scavenging. People love helping and get pleasure from doing someone else a good turn.

Air locks

You need something to cover the mouth of your narrow-necked second stage fermentation vessel.

Shops stock items called air locks, or fermentation locks. They fit into bored cork or rubber bungs, which are also sold and fasten into the tops of 1 gallon (4½ litres) glass jars, or demijohns. They also fit large spirit bottles.

You fill air locks with water, or sulphite solution (sodium metabisulphite mixed with water, see page 31) to keep out insects and bacteria. Carbon dioxide gas produced during fermentation escapes by bubbling through the liquid.

Bubbles become less frequent as wine yeast converts natural sugar (fructose and glucose) and processed household sugar (sucrose) in your wine to alcohol. When bubbling stops altogether, it is an indication that fermentation has ceased; however, you still have to taste the wine to see if it is sweet and therefore not fully fermented, or dry (non-sweet) and finished fermenting as described from page 58.

Air locks are useful gadgets, but not essential. They are made of glass or plastic. Glass air locks soon shatter and can cut you badly. Plastic ones last longer but tend to crack or split eventually and have to be replaced.

Sheets of polythene provide perfectly adequate covering and as everything comes wrapped in polythene of one sort or another nowadays, there is no problem getting a continuous, free supply. Clingfilm and small bags and wrappers are ideal. Plastic carrier bags – the type you collect from supermarkets – can be trimmed with scissors into usable squares. It is only necessary for the polythene to completely cover the mouth of your narrow-necked fermentation vessel.

To do this cut a 7 inch (178mm) square of polythene; smooth it tightly across the top of your narrow-necked fermentation vessel and down the neck. Secure the polythene around the neck with two elastic bands, string or strong thread.

The polythene covering releases harmless carbon dioxide gas given off during fermentation by expanding with the pressure of gas and stretching at the point where it is fastened by elastic bands, string or thread, enabling the gas to force its way out. At the same time the polythene keeps out insects, dust and airborne bacteria.

There are many other satisfactory alternatives to the commercial air lock. A plug of cotton wool pushed into the top of your narrow-necked fermentation vessel makes an excellent air lock. As does a clean piece of cloth, or even an extra-strong paper tissue.

In wine making, the simplest and most obvious devices are often the least costly and the best.

NEVER fasten screw caps on your fermentation vessel.

Bungs

Buy cork or rubber bungs to seal your narrow-necked 1 gallon (4½ litres) storage vessels during the clearing and maturing stage (after fermentation is complete).

Cork bungs come in various sizes from 1 inch (25mm) diameter to 5 inches (127mm) diameter. Standard sizes fit most 1 gallon (4½ litres) jars, bottles and containers but if necessary, shape them to fit your storage vessels with a modelling knife or file, and glasspaper.

NEVER fasten screw caps on your storage vessels.

Corks, caps and stoppers

Corks, plastic caps and cork and plastic stoppers are the next things to look out for.

Some sherry bottles come with reusable stoppers, as do sparkling wine and Champagne bottles.

Make sure you sterilise and rinse them before reuse. *(See page 66).*

Corks bored into by a corkscrew must be thrown away,

because the hole might become infected and spoil the wine.

Corks, plastic caps and cork and plastic stoppers can be bought. Plastic caps and cork and plastic stoppers are reusable, once sterilised and rinsed.

When using caps or stoppers, you must store bottles of wine upright. There is no disadvantage in this.

NEVER fasten screw caps on bottles.

Occasionally, a small fermentation of residual natural sugar (fructose and glucose) or household sugar (sucrose) takes place in wine after it appears to have finished fermenting – unless potassium sorbate is added to the wine, see page 59. (See also chemical free methods, page 48.) Bungs, corks, caps and stoppers can blow off. Screw capped fermentation or storage vessels, and or bottles, may explode!

If you want to display wine in a rack, or store wine bottles stacked on their sides, you must fit conventional straight sided corks driven into necks of wine bottles with a home made flogger (see page 77) or a commercial hand corker, or lever action corking machine.

Sunken, straight sided corks have to be removed with a corkscrew and discarded, unless you acquire a butler's aid, or

'Butler's aid'.

wiggle and twist style of cork remover. These can be bought in home brew shops and some chemists. They consist of two blades of fine steel fixed into a handle. The blades are forced down either side of the cork and it is wiggled out of the neck intact.

The cork should be undamaged and may be sterilised, rinsed and used repeatedly.

Funnel
A funnel is the next item of equipment you will find indispensable.

Nylon or plastic ones are best and a 4 inch (102mm) to 6 inch (152mm) diameter mouth is about the right size.

If you have not got one and do not want to beg, borrow, or buy one, you can make your own.

Using a pair of scissors or modelling knife, cut an empty long-necked polythene bottle a third of the way down from its shoulder. And you have your funnel.

Straining cloth
A straining cloth is essential. Muslin is excellent, as is an old pair of nylons or tights, trimmed with scissors.

Remember to sterilise your muslin or scissor trimmed nylons or tights in a cup or dish of sulphite solution (sodium metabisulphite mixed with water, see page 31) and then rinse in cold water before use.

Measuring jug and scales
These are useful pieces of equipment. A measuring jug is necessary for accurately measuring quantities of liquid, flowers and herbs. Ordinary kitchen scales are adequate for weighing fruit, grain and vegetables.

Spread it round
Always let your friends know you are taking up wine making. Tell them about the sort of things you are looking for and ask them to keep an eye open for suitable items.

Put it on a business footing by offering a share in the finished product. You will be amazed at the diligence with which they seek out odds and bits that prove invaluable.

After gaining experience and confidence you will want to start building a cellar of fine wines. With this in mind, keep a look out for useful equipment to set aside for use when your neighbour makes a gift of some of his bumper crop of apples, or your greengrocer offers over-ripe fruit at give away prices.

If you become really keen you can put a card in a shop window listing items you want, or place an ad. in the local paper, offering to collect. It is surprising what people have stowed away and gladly offload for free, if someone collects.

When you are new to the craft of wine making, make wines in 1 gallon (4½ litres) quantities and later on, having sampled a wide range and decided upon your favourites, you may like to produce particular wines in large batches – if only to keep pace with bottles emptied by your growing circle of sociable and attentive friends.

4

Safety and Cleanliness

Never ferment wine in earthenware crocks with a lead glaze. A white pottery glaze is all right.

Never use metal containers for fermenting wine.

There is a chance acid and alcohol in the wine might draw harmful chemicals from lead and metal and it is not worth risking headaches and nausea.

Use only non-toxic polythene containers made for wine making and brewing, or recommended by the manufacturer for food use, or polythene containers that held food or soft drink.

Never use any vessel which has held a poisonous chemical.

If in doubt, leave it out!

Never fasten screw caps on glass storage vessels or bottles. Occasionally, a small fermentation of residual natural sugar (fructose and glucose) or household sugar (sucrose) occurs in maturing wine. Corks can pop out but screw-capped glass storage vessels and bottles may explode!

Make sure all equipment intended for use is thoroughly clean and sterilised. (See next chapter.)

Remove spots of bacteria from empty fermentation and storage vessels and bottles by washing in a mixture of warm water and washing-up liquid before sterilising them.

To remove unwanted labels from bottles, soak the bottles in warm water. Smear a dab of washing-up liquid on the label for quick results. A few always need scraping off with a knife.

Stubborn stains and mould at the bottom of bottles come away if soaked in neat bleach. A bottle brush is worth having. After soaking, washing and sterilising *rinse everything with warm water*.

Mop up spilled wine as soon as possible. It collects

Bottle brush.

bacteria and the smell of wine attracts the vinegar fly
(Drosophila Melanogaster).

Keep your wine closely covered at all stages of its
development.

5

Sterilising Equipment

All wine making equipment must be sterilised before use to kill bacteria and prevent possible infection of your wine.

To sterilise equipment buy sodium metabisulphite from your chemist or home brew shop – ½ lb (227gms) lasts a fair time.

Sulphite solution
Make the above powder into liquid sulphite solution by stirring 1 oz (28gms) of sodium metabisulphite into 1 pint (½ litre) of warm water. Store it in a stoppered bottle.

This chemical is available in the more expensive form of Campden tablets. Nine crushed Campden tablets dissolved in 1 pint (½ litre) of warm water makes up the sulphite solution.

Do not breathe the sulphur dioxide fumes given off when the chemical is mixed with water. They are unpleasant and cause momentary discomfort.

Swill out fermentation and storage vessels and bottles with sulphite solution before using them; pour the solution back into its bottle and seal with a stopper. It remains potent for months and only needs replacing as its quantity diminishes through usage.

All items of equipment may be sterilised with sulphite solution. A mug or dish of sulphite solution provides a handy sterilising dip. A clean cloth, soaked in sulphite solution, can be used to wipe and sterilise large pieces of equipment.

Rinse sterilised items with water to remove traces of the solution before using them.

6
Storage

Finding room
Never worry about having insufficient room for making and
storing wine. Have a look round your home. There are
corners, cupboards and shelves in every size of residence
where fermenting and maturing wine may be hidden out of
sight.

Finding places to store wine is a matter of initiative. I
knew a woman fascinated by the vast range of colours of
country wines. She decorated her 1 gallon (4½ litres) clear
glass storage vessels with brightly coloured collages made
from varnished pictures cut from magazines. Each collage
was arranged so the natural colour of the wine reflected
through carefully positioned gaps and she used them as
functional ornaments.

The overall effect was interesting and uniquely beautiful. If you have a cupboard under the stairs, a shed or space under the roof, you have no storage problems.

Shelving can be organised to hold large amounts of wine – fermenting, maturing and bottled, but make sure it is strong enough to support the weight.

I have seen bottles kept in a suitcase in a bed-sit with wine for drinking displayed in a rack. A design for an easily assembled bottle rack is included in this book, on page 78.

Storage vessels

Fermentation vessels for the 1st stage may be made of any non-toxic material and all sorts of containers can be used successfully to ferment wine.

This does not apply to the 2nd fermentation stage, when narrow-necked vessels are essential to keep out insects and bacteria, or to the storage vessels used thereafter in which the wine clears and matures.

Storage vessels should also be narrow-necked so that only a small surface area of wine is in contact with air.

Small quantities of air occasionally admitted to wine during storage improve its quality, but continuous absorption of air makes wine taste bland and insipid.

Glass vessels are best for storage because air cannot penetrate glass. Vessels made from plastic or polythene less than 2mm thick allow maturing wine to absorb air through the plastic or polythene and this adversely affects the quality of the wine.

Wine matures better in bulk. One gallon (4½ litres) achieves a finer quality than one bottle. Keep maturing wine in 1 gallon (4½ litres) vessels for at least the minimum period suggested in recipes before bottling.

Where to store

After your wine has finished fermenting and been transferred to a storage vessel to mature, keep it somewhere cool, out of direct sunlight. Wine subject to constant high temperatures may take on a 'cooked' flavour. This is desirable in wines of madeira-like quality and is not unpleasant. The popularity of madeira wine testifies to its acceptability. But it may not be to your taste.

Direct sunlight fades the rich colour of red wine stored in transparent vessels. Keep red wine in coloured, or tinted glass vessels, or stored in a dark place, or cover with sheets of taped newspaper.

Coloured or tinted glass storage vessels and bottles are perfect for red wine and should be used whenever possible.

Maturing Wines

Most wine and particularly red wine, throws sediment as it clears and matures in storage.

If a heavy sediment forms at the bottom of the storage vessel – to a depth of more than ¼ inch (6mm), pour or syphon the wine off its sediment into a sterilised, rinsed container and cover. Clean, sterilise and rinse the storage vessel and pour back the wine. Top up with another wine of similar flavour and colour, or cold water to keep the vessel filled to the neck (see page 63).

Admitting air to your wine briefly once every five months or so, improves its quality.

Where there is only a negligible sediment and pouring or syphoning the wine off its sediment is not necessary, you may put a small amount of air into the wine by removing 1 pint (½ litre) of wine and immediately pouring it back.

Remember to sterilise and rinse utensils before use.

Many wines are drinkable a few months after they have finished fermenting, but keep your wine in 1 gallon (4½ litres) storage vessels for as long as possible. Only bottle wine two or three months before you intend to start drinking it.

After bottling, wine needs two or three months to use up excess air absorbed during bottling and condition itself before being sampled. Wine improves considerably in the bottle for six months and then its rate of improvement slows.

All country wines continue improving but do not mature indefinitely. Depending on the blend of ingredients: white wine improves in quality for up to five years; red wine gains in quality for up to nine years; sweet wines improve longer than dry wines and have a greater life span.

After your wine reaches its peak of perfection, it begins a very slow decline. Recipes in this book give you an idea of when to expect your wine to reach peak perfection.

Heavy-bodied red wine, due to its naturally high level of tannin and acid, sometimes continues maturing for up to fourteen years, but I doubt whether many people would want to wait that long before enjoying it.

A friend of mine made 1 gallon (4½ litres) of elderberry wine when his first child was born and resisted the temptation to drink it until she celebrated her eighteenth birthday, by which time its excellence had to be tasted to be believed.

Storing bottles

Bottles of wine are traditionally stored on their sides to ensure corks are permanently moist and swollen to prevent drying and cracking.

There is no reason why bottles should not be stored upright. The cork is unlikely to crack if covered securely with polythene cut into a 4 inch (102mm) square; smoothed over the top of the bottle and fastened around the neck with two elastic bands, string, or strong thread. (*Two* elastic bands are recommended in case one perishes and snaps.)

Checks

Check stored wine is clearly labelled, or you forget what is where.

Keep an eye on bungs and corks to see they are firmly in place, especially in hot weather.

One 4 inch (102mm) – 7 inch (178mm) square of polythene smoothed over corks and bungs, and secured around the necks of bottles or storage vessels with *two* elastic bands, string or strong thread, permits the cork or bung to rise and release carbon dioxide gas produced in the unlikely event of a secondary fermentation of residual household sugar (sucrose) or natural sugar (fructose and glucose) sometimes present in the wine, without the cork or bung flying off and exposing the wine to possible infection. The use of potassium sorbate (page 47) can prevent such a secondary fermentation.

You can refit the cork or bung immediately you discover it has come loose.

7
Collecting Ingredients

Best results are achieved by using freshly gathered ingredients. However, if you live in a town and do not fancy a trip into parks or countryside, you will be pleased to learn that many flowers, herbs and some fruit, notably elderberries and sloes, can be bought dried from health food and home brew stockists. The packs are not expensive.

Avoid natural ingredients you know have been treated with insecticide.

If you suspect they may have been, rinse them in cold water before use, or before drying and preserving them.

Gathering fruit, flowers, herbs and leaves is fun and an excuse, if you need one, to wander along hedgerows of

country lanes and through fields and beautiful meadows with carrier bag, rucksack and identification guide, looking for natural ingredients for your wines.

Children enjoy gathering, especially if their effort is rewarded by payment at piece-work rates. A picnic by the edge of a stream in a leafy glade also rewards them with a relaxing highlight to a pleasant day out. They must be warned not to trespass, or trample on farmers' crops.

Many flowers are accessible in towns. Rose petals spill in large amounts onto grass in parks and lie awaiting collection.

Dandelions are everywhere, coming up between paving slabs and flourishing on grass verges at roadsides.

Tree leaves abound and tea leaves, in bags or loose, are used by everyone and make several styles of wine.

You may know someone prepared to supply a few kilograms of fruit or vegetables in return for bottles of wine.

Fruit and vegetables are easily grown if you have access to a kitchen garden or allotment. Allotments are available in cities and towns, and applications should be made to the local council.

Look out for special offers on fruit and vegetables at your green-grocers. Over-ripe fruit is usually reduced in price and ideal for making wine.

To extract the most scent, flavour and natural goodness from fresh flowers and herbs, collect them in full bloom.

Mid-morning of a dry day is preferable. Time your picking so dew has evaporated from the flowers and the sun had not yet become hot enough to dry oils from their leaves. Early evening, before dew forms, is also suitable for gathering flowers and herbs.

Blooms should be handled carefully and spread out loosely, taking care not to press them down too heavily.

Fruit is best fully ripe and vegetables should be newly dug. Leaves should be green.

Measuring

Some wine makers like to take a plastic or polythene measuring jug and mini spring-balance with them when gathering ingredients, so they know when to stop picking.

Berries and fruit can be weighed in a plastic carrier bag, suspended from a spring-balance. Flowers, herbs and leaves should be pressed down lightly in a measuring jug. Remove stems from flowers and herbs for an accurate measurement, or make allowance for them.

Use fresh
Use fresh ingredients. For best results, start work on turning fresh ingredients into wine as soon as you get them home.

8
Plants Best Avoided

Wine may safely be made from many plants but some are best avoided. Not all plants listed here are poisonous, some might leave you unaffected or only slightly nauseous – a few could kill.

Your Deadly Nightshade Liqueur or Sparkling Toadstool Surprise may look nice in the bottle but if you serve them to guests your circle of friends reclines and declines until you find yourself helping the police with their enquiries.

It is safest sticking to known recipes but if determined to blaze new trails in progressive country wine making, at least check ingredients carefully to make sure you are not perfecting a poison to which there is no antidote.

Avoid all plants sprayed with insecticide.

Before picking (with permission) from a flower border or the local woods, read this list. It is not exhaustive but gives an idea of what NOT to ferment.

Anemone, azalea; Bluebell, buttercup; Clematis, columbine, crocus, crowfoot, cyclamen; Daffodil, dahlia; Foxglove, fungi; Geranium, gladiolus; Hemlock, hyacinth; Iris; Lobelia, lupins; Narcisus, nightshade of all varieties; Peony, poppy; Rhubarb leaves (leaves only); Snowdrop, sweet pea; Tobacco, tulip.

9
Preserving Ingredients

Fresh fruit, flowers, herbs, leaves and vegetables are ideal for making high quality, nutritious wines. It makes sense to gather, preserve and store them when plentiful, for use when short of fresh ingredients for wine making.

Drying flowers, herbs, and leaves
If you think flowers, herbs or leaves may have been treated with insecticide, rinse them in cold water before drying them.

Traditionally, flowers and herbs were strung together in bunches and hung somewhere dark, dry, warm and airy until they were crisp and brittle. An attic, airing cupboard, darkened shed, garage, or under-stairs cupboard are suitable places.

Here is another effective way of drying them. You can spread flowers, herbs and leaves evenly on a baking tray and pop it in a very slow oven heated to 29°C (85°F). The flowers, herbs or leaves should be dry after about ninety minutes.

A less satisfactory but more economical way, is to spread them evenly on a baking tray and put the tray in your oven after a meal has been cooked, making use of the reducing heat. Do not put the tray in your oven until the temperature has cooled to about 38°C (100°F). You will need to repeat this procedure several times before petals or leaves are crisp and brittle.

Flowers, herbs and leaves are delicate and need treating carefully. They are spoilt by long exposure to excessive light, damp or heat.

When the petals or leaves are dry, crisp and brittle, crumble them from their stems and store in a sealed jar or air-tight polythene container.

Remember to label the contents and keep them away from heat and strong light.

Dried flowers, herbs and leaves stay in good condition for a year, then their quality begins to fade.

2 oz (56gms) of dried flowers, herbs or leaves is equal to approximately 1 quart (1 litre) freshly picked and 4 oz (113gms) dried is equal to 2 quarts (2¼ litres) freshly picked.

Depending on the recipe you are following and the strength of flavour you require in your finished wine, 2 oz (56gms) to 4 oz (113gms) is sufficient for 1 gallon (4½ litres) of wine.

Deep freezing fruit and vegetables
Deep freezing is the most satisfactory way of preserving fruit and although scalding of vegetables is normally required, much of the flavour and nutritional value is retained and passed on in the fermented wine. Your instruction booklet tells you the best way of preparing ingredients for your freezer. A deep freeze offers you the opportunity to bulk buy fruit and vegetables at low prices and capitalize on your forward planning whenever it suits you.

Pulp bottling of fruit
A good idea if you have storage jars and space to store them. The main disadvantage with this method is that some of the fruit's natural goodness disappears in steam as it simmers. Your wine may also take a month or two longer than normal to clear, because simmered fruit releases pectin, which clouds wine.

Peel and core apples. Remove stems, stalks and stones from apricots, cherries, peaches etc. Simmer the prepared fruit in a covered saucepan with just enough water to prevent burning; reduce to pulp, pour into warmed jars, fasten lids and seal. Check next day to make sure lids are tight and there is a vacuum. When using jars with screw bands, smear the thread with vaseline or olive oil before storing.

Beetroot, Carrots and Parsnips
Main crop varieties may be left in the ground until needed but if you want to keep them through the winter, or bulk buy at bargain prices and do not wish to use them all at once, you can pack them in boxes between layers of dry soil, sand or peat and store in a cool, frost free place.

10
Wine Records

Keep records. No matter how good your memory, you soon lose track of recipes followed.

Often, deliberate or chance variation of a recipe produces an excellent wine, much to your taste, which you wish to duplicate. Without an adequate record of how the wine was made you have no hope of repeating your triumph. You can buy record cards for winemaking from your homebrew stockist, or make your own.

An exercise book or a few sheets of paper pinned, stapled or clipped together is all you need. The pages could be ruled and set out thus:

Name of wine:
Ingredients:
Date Fermentation Started:
Date Fermentation Ceased:
Date Racked Into Storage Vessel:
Date Bottled:
Remarks:

The remarks section should include information likely to be useful when the recipe is repeated. For instance, when and where the ingredients were gathered, how they were prepared, under what conditions they were fermented and stored, tasting notes etc.

When sampling a maturing wine, draw a small amount from the storage vessel into a sterilised, *rinsed* pipette, by placing it in the wine and covering the top end with your forefinger. Then transfer the sample to a glass. The bulk of wine is undisturbed and only an insignificant quantity removed.

Wine making pipettes are sold but the plastic tube of an

empty biro or felt tip pen cleaned, sterilised and *rinsed* makes a serviceable pipette.

Detailed and critical observation and assessment of the wine making process adds interest to the craft, teaches a great deal and suggests improvements and short cuts.

Informed and intelligent practice makes for perfection.

<u>Name of wine</u>: Dandelion

<u>Ingredients</u>: Dandelions – 2 quarts (2¼ litres) of fresh heads,
Sultanas – 1 lb (½ Kg).
Orange Blossom Honey – 1 lb (½ Kg.),
White grape juice, pure – 3½ pints (2 litres)
Marmite – ¼ teaspoon,
Tea, strong – ½ cup,
Oranges – 2,
C.W.E. Formula 67 yeast starter bottle.

<u>Date Fermentation Started</u>: 23rd. April.

<u>Date Fermentation ceased</u>: Finished by 20th. May.
Double checked 4th June.

<u>Date racked into storage vessel</u>: 4th June.

<u>Date bottled</u>: 4th February (9½ months after
fermentation started.)

<u>Remarks</u>:

23rd April.   Traditional Day for making
Dandelion wine. St. George's Day. Picked
dandelions 11.30 a.m. on common
opposite Rose and Crown. Cool day,
flowers open; dew evaporated from
leaves. Prepared ingredients according

to my usual recipe. Added C.W.E. Formula
67 wine yeast from starter bottle at 4.00pm.
Used covered plastic bucket for stage I
fermentation. Put in shed. Warm place
on a sunny day.

24th April: Warm in shed. Vigorous fermentation.
Lots of bubbling and frothing.
Stirred thoroughly.

30th April: Less bubbling and frothing. Fermentation
slowing. Have stirred twice daily.

4th May: The 10 days for stage I are up. Wine tastes
sweet and musty! Dandelion, tea, orange
and honey flavours clashing together.
Poured wine through muslin covered funnel
into 1 gallon (4½ litres) clear glass
fermentation vessel for stage 2 fermentation.
Topped wine up to 1 gallon (4½ litres)

5th May: Warm today. Bubbles rising quickly to
surface. Fermenting strongly.

15th May: Fewer bubbles. Wine a lighter shade near
the surface. Starting to clear.

11

Chemical-free Wine

Superb country wines have been made for centuries without the assistance of chemicals. It follows that it is not essential to add *any* chemical to your wine and if you want to produce chemical-free, natural country wines, you can.

What the two chemicals most commonly added in tiny quantities are for, is described first, followed by ways to work without them for the purist. However, their use can save time and worry and there is little evidence that such small amounts could cause harm; in the working methods described in this book their possible advantageous use is therefore included.

A few processed or manufactured ingredients on sale also contain chemical additives which are regarded as harmless but again, ways the purist can avoid them easily are described.

Sodium metabisulphite

a) *For hygiene – kills bacteria*

For maximum hygiene, sterilise all your equipment before use with sulphite solution (sodium metabisulphite mixed with water, see page 31). Then *rinse away* traces of sulphite solution with cold water.

b) *To stun wine yeast and assist clearing after fermentation finishes but before racking*

1 level *tea*spoon (5ml) of sulphite solution (sodium metabisulphite mixed with water, see page 31) or 1 crushed Campden tablet (sodium metabisulphite) may be added to 1 gallon (4½ litres) of wine after it has finished fermenting to stun any active wine yeast and encourage speedy clearing, see page 58.

You need NOT add sodium metabisulphite. Wine yeast settles and the wine clears naturally but takes a little more time – probably three to five weeks longer.

c) *To use up excess air and encourage clearing in fermented wine once it is racked into the storage vessel*

Where it has not been helpful or desired as in (b) above, and used already, the same quantity of this substance added to your wine once it has been racked from the fermentation vessel into a storage vessel can be a help clearing and using up excess air absorbed during racking, see page 59.

Sulphite solution or a Campden tablet can also be added to the wine a second time just before bottling. This will help use up excess air absorbed during the bottling and to accelerate its conditioning in the bottle, making it ready for drinking two months after bottling, see page 66.

However, you need NOT use sulphite solution or a Campden tablet at all, either after racking into a storage vessel, or before bottling. Your wine uses up excess air and clears naturally, and only takes a little longer. Wine in a storage vessel takes a month to use up naturally the air absorbed during the racking but this will not affect its time in storage, which remains the same.

Wine bottled without addition of sulphite solution or a Campden tablet, needs three months to condition in the bottle before drinking, instead of two months, see page 67.

Potassium sorbate

Inhibits wine yeast from further activity in fermented wine either while stored to clear and mature, or in the bottled wine.

Potassium sorbate added when fermentation is thought to be complete and before racking into a storage vessel to mature and clear is like an extra insurance to make certain no bungs or corks are blown out by a chance secondary fermentation of residual natural sugar (fructose and glucose) and/or household sugar (sucrose); this is described fully on page 59.

You need NOT add potassium sorbate to your wine after it has finished fermenting. A secondary fermentation is unlikely to occur if you follow instructions in the recipes. Wine yeast usually ferments all the natural sugar (fructose and glucose) and/or household sugar (sucrose) in wine without problems.

To be extra safe, instead of adding potassium sorbate (or as well if you like), you can cover corks, stoppers and bungs. Use polythene cut into a 4 inch (102mm) – 7 inch (178mm) square smoothed over the top of the storage vessel or bottle and fastened securely around the neck with two elastic bands, string, or strong thread.

The bung, cork or stopper rises to release carbon dioxide gas produced by fermentation if any secondary one does occur but does not fly off and expose the wine to possible infection. You can re-fasten the bung, cork or stopper immediately you discover it is loose.

Chemicals in ingredients

Concentrated wine making grape juice

Concentrated wine making grape juice often contains chemical additives; usually: citric acid, diammonium phosphate, flavouring, glucose syrup, lactic acid, saccharin, sulphur dioxide and tannic acid.

Use chemical-free, pure grape juice, as directed in recipes.

Marmite: yeast extract

Marmite and yeast extract usually contain some flavouring and salt. Use ¼ *tea*spoon of pure malt extract instead, if you prefer.

Dried wine yeast compound

Some dried wine yeast compounds contain tiny amounts of ammonium chloride, ammonium phosphate dibasic and sugar (sucrose).

Check listed ingredients carefully.

Liquid wine yeast – living wine yeast, cultured in a liquid medium in a phial, is the pure, natural alternative to dried wine yeast compound.

12
Sugar-free Wines

Refined sugar cane and sugar beet, familiar to us as processed household sugar (sucrose) may be replaced in recipes by a combination of the natural sugar (fructose and glucose) found in pure honey, plus pure grape juice, or concentrated wine making grape juice, and extra raisins (dried black grapes) and/or sultanas (dried white grapes). Full instructions for making country wines without adding household sugar (sucrose) are given in the recipe section of this book.

You can buy pure honey and pure grape juice from your health food stockist.

Concentrated wine making grape juice is available from your home brew stockist. As well as concentrated grape juice, it often contains some chemicals, usually: glucose syrup, lactic acid, saccharin, sulphur dioxide and tannic acid. If you prefer to work additive-free use only pure grape juice. Details are included in recipes.

Table of equivalents

Approximate natural sugar (fructose and glucose) content of pure honey; pure grape juice; concentrated wine making grape juice; raisins and sultanas:

1 lb (454g) of pure honey contains about 14 oz (397g) of natural sugar.

1 pint (½ litre) of pure grape juice (red or white) contains about 4 oz (113g) of natural sugar.

1 pint (½ litre) of concentrated wine making grape juice (red or white) contains about 1 lb (454g) of natural sugar.

1 lb (454g) of raisins or sultanas contains about 10½ oz (298g) of natural sugar.

Because the amount of natural sugar (fructose and glucose) in these items is bound to vary occasionally, figures can only be approximate but they are accurate enough for our purpose.

With this table of equivalents it is possible to devise a balanced list of ingredients supplying a natural sugar (fructose and glucose) alternative to processed household sugar (sucrose).

Dried wine yeast compound

Some dried wine yeast compounds contain tiny amounts of sugar (sucrose). Check listed ingredients carefully. Liquid natural wine yeast, sold in phials, is a pure, living alternative to dried wine yeast.

13
Honey in Wine

For centuries pure honey was an invaluable ingredient in country wines, endowing them with its unique qualities and supplying natural sugar (fructose and glucose) for wine yeast to ferment to alcohol.

Pure honey provides country wine with extra flavour, a superbly rich, full, smoothness and improves or bestows an impressive bouquet.

The nutritional value and healing powers credited to honey, are added to those of other ingredients in country wine. Combined, they present a strong package of natural goodness in matured, ready to drink wine.

Selecting honey

Use only pure honey. Blended honey is cheaper, but characterless and honey spreads include adjuncts which taste unpleasant in wine. Any pure honey may be used. The choice is yours. Excellent honeys are imported from many countries, from Australia to Romania. They are all worth sampling in wine. Recipes in this book suggest a particular honey suitable for use with each wine but please experiment with your favourites.

Each type of honey produces subtle differences in the finished wine. Select honey with a flavour you feel will complement the wine.

Try light coloured, delicate, single blossom honeys with flower wines. Dark coloured honey tastes good with strongly flavoured red wines. Mixed blossom honey may be used with any wine.

Beware of Australian eucalyptus blossom honey. The eucalyptus flavour is unacceptable to many people.

Heather honey gives its distinctive flavour to wine but be

certain you like heather honey before using it.

English honey is full flavoured. Imported honeys are usually milder.

It makes no difference to wine whether honey is liquid or crystalline.

Honey for health

Nectar, collected by bees from plants to make honey, includes medicinal properties associated with the plants and those healing qualities are contained in honey.

Honey is highly nutritious and a prime source of valuable natural acids, enzymes, mineral salts, proteins, trace elements and vitamins.

From the earliest times, honey was accorded special therapeutic and healing powers and has been used to effect miraculous cures, rejuvenate and prolong life.

Honey's ancient association with love and romance is reflected in the word 'honeymoon', a reference to the mead and honeyed wine traditionally drunk by a couple for one month after their wedding. Honeymoon gets its meaning from honey (love) and moon (romance for a lunar month). Honey has long been regarded as a natural aphrodisiac.

Put some in

If you intend using processed household sugar (sucrose) in country recipes, try replacing some of the household sugar (sucrose) with pure honey. It will improve the quality of your wine.

1 lb (454g) of pure honey equals about 14 oz (397g) of household sugar.

14
Starting A Fermentation

Fermentation is the action of wine yeast working on natural sugar (fructose and glucose) present in some ingredients and in honey and/or on processed household sugar (sucrose) to produce alcohol.

Wine yeast
You have a choice of forms of wine yeast. It is sold as dried granules in tubs and single packets, or tablets in tubes and as liquid natural wine yeast, a pure wine yeast living in a liquid or jelly medium in a phial. Quantities required per unit of liquid wine being made are always marked on wine yeast sold in home brew specialists.

Many styles of wine yeast are available, from Chianti to Tokay, each contributing its own subtle characteristics to your wine.

You can experiment with these if you wish, but an all-purpose wine yeast is suitable for country wines.

Wine yeast becomes active as soon as it is added to a sugary substance and may be put straight into your bucket or bin of prepared ingredients. However, manufacturers recommend the best way to activate their particular types of wine yeast and it is wise to follow their instructions.

Whichever form or style of wine yeast you decide to use, there is one way to activate and nurture it that could save you buying any more – it is to make up a wine yeast starter bottle.

Wine yeast starter bottle
Sterilise a standard size wine bottle and plastic or polythene funnel with sulphite solution (sodium metabisulphite mixed with water, see page 31) and *rinse* with water. Place the funnel in the bottle and, following the manufacturer's

instructions, measure enough wine yeast to ferment 1 gallon (4½ litres) of wine, into the empty bottle. Add ½ pint (284ml) of cold water and 1 level *table*spoon of pure lemon or orange juice. Pour 5 fl oz (142ml) of boiling water into a cup and dissolve 2 level *table*spoons of pure malt extract (which contains nutrients and natural sugar – maltose). Cover and allow to cool. Then pour into bottle. Top up with cold water to within 3 inches (76mm) of the top of the bottle and cover with a 4 inch (102mm) square of sterilised, *rinsed* polythene secured around the bottle neck with an elastic band, string or strong thread. Keep the bottle in a warm place for 48 hours so that the wine yeast can multiply in the acid/nutrient/sugary solution. After 48 hours, store the wine yeast starter bottle in your fridge or a cool place.

It is now ready for use.

Using your wine yeast starter bottle

To start a fermentation, pour ¾ of the wine yeast starter bottle into your bucket or bin of prepared ingredients. This is enough to start 1 gallon (4½ litres) fermenting within 48 hours. To your ¼ full starter bottle, add fresh pure lemon or orange juice and pure malt extract – in the same quantities you used before; top up with cold water to within 3 inches (76mm) of the top of the bottle, cover with a square of sterilised, *rinsed* polythene and keep in a warm place for 7 days. During this time the wine yeast re-establishes a strong colony and after 7 days you may use ¾ of the starter bottle to begin another fermentation.

Providing the wine yeast starter bottle is kept in sterile conditions it will not be infected by bacteria and can be topped up and used indefinitely.

If you do not want to use it straight away, the wine yeast remains potent in the bottle for up to a year.

Keep it in your fridge, or somewhere cool.

FERMENTATION

Fermentation is conducted in two distinct stages. The first in a covered bucket, bin or suitable wide-mouthed container. The second in a covered narrow-necked 1 gallon (4½ litres) fermentation vessel.

Remember to sterilise *and rinse* all equipment used.

Fermentation stage 1

Ingredients are fermented together for 10 days.

Within 48 hours fermentation becomes vigorous and there is some frothing and foaming. Allow for this by leaving at least 2 inches (51mm) – 4 inches (102mm) head space at the top of your bucket or bin. The wider it is the less space you need leave. Fermentation slows and settles after a few days and is strong but steady by the tenth day.

Fermentation stage one.

Air space is desirable because air is used by wine yeast in the first stage of fermentation to establish a thriving colony.

Making wine makes enemies. The worst is the tiny vinegar fly (Drosophila Melanogaster). Attracted by the sweet smell of fermentation, it dives into uncovered wine and bacteria the fly carries turn your wine to vinegar.

Some enemies are invisible. Fungal spores and bacterial cells float in the air and can infect wine in its early stages. Keep vessels covered.

Covering your bucket or bin
Either use a lid, or a large sheet of sterilised, *rinsed* polythene, or a sterilised and *rinsed out* clean cloth, secured around the edge of your vessel by elastic, string or strong thread.

Once fermenting, a cloud of carbon dioxide gas covers your wine, discouraging the vinegar fly (Drosophila Melanogaster) and airborne bacteria from approaching.

After a few days your wine reaches 4% alcohol per volume (7% proof). This level of alcohol kills bacteria and your wine should be safe but keep it covered.

Fermentation stage 2
After 10 days the fermenting wine is racked by scooping up wine and solids in a sterilised, *rinsed* jug, mug or cup and straining through sterilised, *rinsed* muslin or scissor trimmed tights into a narrow-necked 1 gallon (4½ litres) fermentation vessel, see page 61. (Solids left in wine after 10 days start decomposing and could taint your wine). Cold water is used for any final top up.

Covering your fermentation vessel
The mouth of your narrow-necked fermentation vessel can be covered with a 7 inch (178mm) square of polythene; smoothed tightly over the top of the vessel and secured around the neck by two elastic bands, string or strong thread, or plugged with a wad of cotton wool, or an air lock fitted into a bored cork or rubber bung and filled with water or sulphite solution (sodium metabisulphite mixed with water, see page 31).

Each of these coverings satisfactorily releases harmless carbon dioxide gas given off during fermentation and keeps out insects and bacteria attracted by the sweet, fruity scent of fermenting wine.

Fermentation is continued with wine only and *no air space*, so wine yeast concentrates on converting natural sugar (fructose and glucose) and/or household sugar (sucrose) to alcohol.

The warmer wine is, the faster it ferments. An even temperature of 18°C (64°F) is ideal.

If you cannot keep your fermentation vessel in the warm you may like to buy a special winemaker's heating tray, or heating belt to fit around your fermentation vessel. Visit your local home brew stockist and see what is available.

If you are a D.I.Y. enthusiast you can easily make your own heating tray from an empty biscuit tin, using a 40 watt bulb positioned inside the tin to provide sufficient warmth to keep your wine fermenting in the coldest weather. However you must make certain the wiring is safe before using it bearing in mind it is possible for the wine to froth over.

During fermentation the chemical reaction between wine yeast and ingredients raises the temperature inside the fermentation vessel higher than the temperature outside and you may take advantage of this by insulating it.

You could ask the knitter in your life for a dinky woollen pullover for your fermentation vessel but newspapers taped around the outside does the trick and a few newspapers or polystyrene tiles placed underneath make a difference.

Do not use pullovers, newspapers, or polystyrene tiles if you are fermenting your wine on a heating tray, or you might have a fire to deal with.

Wine can take from four weeks to three months to finish fermenting, depending on the temperature, the amount of natural sugar (fructose and glucose) and/or household sugar (sucrose) to be fermented and the balance of ingredients, nutrients and acid.

Never be in too much of a hurry.

There is no disadvantage in a slow fermentation and if content to wait longer for your wines, you may leave them anywhere to ferment.

The steadier a fermentation, the finer the quality of a finished wine.

Because wine yeast converts the natural sugar (fructose and glucose) and/or household sugar (sucrose) to alcohol, the volume of wine shrinks. To compensate for this, top up fermenting wine with cold water or wine of similar flavour and colour, as directed in recipes.

Let wines ferment to dryness (non-sweetness). By fermenting all natural sugar (fructose and glucose) and/or household sugar (sucrose) in your wine completely, you avoid the slight risk of bungs, corks and stoppers popping out of storage vessels and bottles through a secondary fermentation of residual natural sugar (fructose and glucose) or household sugar (sucrose). How to deal with this problem if it does arise is dealt with below.

Judging when fermentation has finished

Watch your wine closely. When there are no bubbles rising to the surface and it looks inactive, check to see if it tastes dry (non-sweet). Pour a little wine into a glass; or draw some into a sterilised, *rinsed* pipette or empty tube from a biro or felt tip pen, by lowering the tube in the wine, placing your forefinger over the open end, lifting the pipette from the fermentation vessel and transferring the wine to a glass.

If it tastes dry – there is no hint of sweetness, no bubbles of carbon dioxide gas and it is not fizzy on the tongue, you may reasonably assume fermentation has finished.

You can double check by fitting a water filled air lock into a bored cork or rubber bung and plugging it into the top of your fermentation vessel. If the wine is still fermenting, bubbles of carbon dioxide gas pass slowly up through the water. If there are no bubbles, fermentation has stopped.

If you are using chemicals (see chapter 11), now add 1 level teaspoon (5ml) of sulphite solution (sodium metabisulphite mixed with water, see page 31) or 1 crushed Campden tablet (sodium metabisulphite) to stun any active wine yeast, which then sinks to the bottom of the fermentation vessel, taking with it bits of suspended pulp and allowing your wine to become clearer before being racked – that is poured or syphoned off its sediment into a storage vessel.

Wait for 2 weeks. If there are no further signs of fermentation, rack the wine into a narrow-necked 1 gallon (4½ litres) storage vessel to clear and mature before bottling, see page 62.

Storage
Another feature of the addition of sodium metabisulphite is that it will absorb excess air collected during the racking process. Even if you did not feel it necessary to use it to help get the pulp to the bottom and wait the two weeks, you may – unless you prefer to work without chemical aids – wish to add it immediately after racking instead. During the storage stage which then follows it will, in addition to clearing excess air, encourage speedy development of the wine's smooth, silky texture, as well as assisting the general progress of clearing and maturing.

Those wine makers who wish to work additive-free will note that wines *do* clear naturally (including losing excess air) without chemical aid and will develop naturally, though perhaps slightly more slowly, without chemical encouragement. Just a few weeks longer are all that is required.

Minimum storage times will be found suggested in each recipe.

Overcoming any secondary fermentation
This phenomenon, you were warned about above on page 58, can occur during the storage stage or even after the wine is bottled. You may choose to remove permanently any slight chance of this happening by the addition of potassium sorbate just before you rack into the storage vessel; or, if you wish chemical-free wine, you can cover the storage vessel neck as described in Chapter 6 and follow the same procedure later on when you bottle the wine (page 68) as an alternative method of overcoming the possible hazard.

Small tubs of potassium sorbate are sold by your local home brew stockist. Use one heaped *tea*spoon (5ml) to each gallon (4½ litres) of wine. Put it in before you rack into the storage vessel but only after you are sure fermentation is finished as explained above.

Sweet or dry wine?
Should you prefer sweet wine, ferment your wine to dryness (non-sweetness); wait until the wine has cleared, matured and been bottled and sweeten it with granulated sugar or

pure honey before serving, see page 71.

This way, you can serve the same wine in differing degrees of dryness or sweetness to suit the taste of individual guests – dry, medium dry, medium sweet, sweet or very sweet.

15
Racking

Racking is a term describing the action of separating wine from its sediment. This may be done by scooping, pouring or syphoning, using a plastic syphon tube about 4 feet (1.2 metres) long.

The method adopted depends on its practicality and your preference.

Watch out – is the fly about?

Watch out for your tiny enemy – the vinegar fly (Drosophila Melanogaster). It is attracted by the scent of fermenting wine. Keep all insects away from wine during racking. Always cover your wine during racking. Always cover your wine securely if called away mid-rack and re-sterilise and *rinse* equipment left unattended before use. Better to be safe than sorry.

Racking after fermentation stage 1

When fermentation stage 1 is completed after 10 days in a bucket, brewing bin or suitable wide-mouthed container, the fermenting wine is racked from its sediment. Use a sterilised, *rinsed* jug, mug or cup to scoop up the mixed wine and solids and strain the wine into a sterilised, *rinsed* narrow-necked glass or plastic, or polythene fermentation vessel through sterilised, *rinsed* muslin or scissor trimmed tights stretched across the mouth of a sterilised, *rinsed* polythene funnel. Strain every drop of wine. Top up with cold water if need.

Cover the fermentation vessel with a 7 inch (178mm) square of sterilised, *rinsed* polythene secured around the neck with two elastic bands, string or strong thread, or plug with cotton wool, or use an air lock fitted into a sterilised, *rinsed* cork or rubber bung and filled with water or sulphite solution (sodium metabisulphite mixed with water, see page 31).

Discard strained solids. If you have a garden, they make good fertilizer. The wine yeast remaining at the bottom of the bucket or wide-mouthed container will have decomposing solids in it and should also be discarded.

Racking after fermentation stage 2

The wine is racked now into a 1 gallon (4½ litres) narrow-necked glass or plastic (2mm thick), or polythene (2mm thick) vessel and stored for the minimum period suggested in the recipe, to allow the wine time to clear and mature before being bottled two or three months prior to drinking.

Sterilise and *rinse* all equipment before use.

Place a plastic or polythene funnel in the mouth of your narrow-necked storage vessel.

If racking the wine by pouring, try not to disturb sediment.

When syphoning, place the fermentation vessel on a surface at a higher level than the storage vessel to be filled.

Position one end of the syphon tubing in the wine slightly above the sediment; suck some wine into the tube and seal the free end with your thumb; then transfer this end in to the mouth of your funnel. When you release your thumb the wine flows from one vessel into the other.

To replace the volume of wine lost in sediment, top up to the neck of your storage vessel with wine of similar colour and flavour from a previously made batch, or cold water.

After racking, fit a sterilised, *rinsed* cork or rubber bung to seal your storage vessel.

Soak cork bungs in a sealed jar filled with sulphite solution (sodium metabisulphite mixed with water, see page 31) for thirty minutes before use. If you are making chemical-free wine you will need to cover the bung as described on page 48.

Keep sediment left in the fermentation vessel if it looks free of solid matter. Wine yeast in the sediment is still strong and potentially active. If you wish, you can swill it out with 1 pint (½ litre) of cold water; pour it into a sterilised, *rinsed*

bucket or wide-mouthed container; add ingredients for a
fresh recipe and get another gallon (4½ litres) of wine off to
an express start.

Sediment may be used for cooking in the same way as
wine.

If there are too many bits in the sediment for your liking,
throw it away.

Racking wine in storage

If wine, as it clears, throws a heavy sediment in storage – to a
depth of more than ¼ inch (6mm), syphon or pour the wine
off its sediment into a sterilised, *rinsed* container; cover
securely, wash out the storage vessel, sterilise and *rinse* it and
then pour back the wine. Top up with wine of similar flavour
and colour, or cold water, to replace the volume lost in
sediment. Keep the storage vessel filled to the neck.

Racking often assists a hazy maturing wine to clear.

Racking wine into bottles

This is the final racking of wine, when it is clear and mature
and is syphoned into sterilised, *rinsed* bottles two or three
months before it is required for drinking, see page 66.

16
Clearing

After wine has finished fermenting, it should be stored in narrow-necked glass or plastic (minimum 2mm thick), or polythene (mininum 2mm thick) vessels and kept in a cool place to clear and mature.

All wines clear on their own if left long enough and an indication of the minimum time required for each wine to clear is given in each recipe. If your wine has matured for the period suggested in the recipe and you want to bottle it, but find it unacceptably hazy, there are ways to speed its clearance.

Many commercial clearing and filtering accessories are sold by home brew stockists, but inexpensive, natural methods often prove just as effective.

Try one or more of these tricks:

Allow two weeks for each method to show signs of working before trying another. Re-seal the storage vessel properly during each attempt covering the bung as explained on page 48 if you are working chemical-free. Quantities are for 1 gallon (4½ litres) of wine.

a) Racking – a second or third racking of wine maturing in a storage vessel is often effective, see page 63. A sudden dose of air admitted to wine helps it stabilise and clear.

b) Remove 1 pint (½ litre) of hazy wine and swap it with 1 pint (½ litre) of clear wine of similar flavour and colour. Clear wine assists hazy wine to clear.

c) Tea, brewed and strained – add 1 level *table*spoon to the wine. Tannin in tea encourages wine to clear.

d) Milk, fresh (no cream) – add 1 level *tea*spoon (5ml) to hazy wine, or ½ *tea*spoon (5ml) of dried skimmed milk mixed into a cupful of the hazy wine and returned to the storage vessel.

e) Eggshells – lightly bake or grill shells of three eggs until dry, then powder them finely and add to the wine. When it has done its job the powder settles with the sediment.

f) Egg white – mix the white of an egg into a cupful of hazy wine and pour back into the storage vessel.

g) Cotton wool – plug a pad of cotton wool into the bottom of a sterilised, rinsed polythene funnel and filter the wine through it into another sterilised, *rinsed* narrow-necked storage vessel. Replace cotton wool if it becomes clogged. Seal the storage vessel securely (as above) with a sterilised, *rinsed* cork or rubber bung and keep somewhere cool to complete clearing.

17
Bottling

1 gallon (4½ litres) of wine fills six-and-a-half standard size wine bottles. Empty half-size wine bottles can usually be acquired from restaurants and wine bars for the asking and are useful for holding the odd half bottle left over from your gallon (4½ litres) of wine.

Assemble the bottles when your wine has cleared and matured in the narrow-necked glass or plastic, or polythene storage vessel for the minimum period suggested in the recipe.

Never fasten screw-caps on bottles.

Soak straight sided corks for twenty-four hours in a sealed jar filled with sulphite solution (sodium metabisulphite mixed with water – see page 31). This sterilises and softens them. Then *rinse* before use.

Soak cork stoppers in a sealed jar filled with sulphite solution for thirty minutes. Stoppers do not need softening and thirty minutes is adequate to kill bacteria in the cork. *Rinse* before using.

Plastic stoppers should be clean and sterilised.

Sterilise and *rinse* your 4 feet (1.2 metre) long plastic syphon tubing. A sterilised, *rinsed* polythene funnel is useful.

Clean the bottles, sterilise with sulphite solution and *rinse* with water.

If you are using chemicals (see chapter 11) add a level *tea*spoon (5ml) of sulphite solution or a crushed Campden tablet (sodium metabisulphite) to the wine before syphoning into bottles. This assists the wine to use up excess air absorbed during bottling and helps ensure it will be ready for drinking after two months in the bottle.

If you are making natural wines, without chemicals, do

not put sulphite solution or a Campden tablet in the wine. Your wine will use up air naturally but takes longer to do so – allow your wine three months to condition in the bottle before enjoying it, instead of two months.

Place the storage vessel on a surface at a higher level than the empty bottles; put one end of the syphon tubing in the wine so it rests just above the sediment and suck some wine into the tube; press your forefinger over the open end. Position the funnel in the neck of the first bottle, hold the syphon tubing in the mouth of the funnel. Remove your forefinger and the wine passes into the bottle. To stop the flow of wine, gently block the end of the syphon tubing with your forefinger.

To simplify bottling, you can buy a small plastic on/off tap to fit into the end of syphon tubing from your home brew stockist.

Repeating this action, fill each bottle with wine to within $2\frac{1}{4}$ inches (57mm) of the top of the bottle. Then seal securely with straight sided corks, or stoppers. When bottles are to be stored upright and you are using cork or plastic stoppers, this operation is simple.

If sinking straight sided corks into the necks of bottles because you wish to store them on their sides or display them in a wine rack, you need a home-made flogger or a commercial hand corker, or lever action corking machine to ram them home. A design for an easily constructed flogger is included in this book on page 77.

Air pressure inside the bottle sometimes forces out a straight sided, sunken cork soon after being driven in. Gently apply pressure with your thumb and push it down again. You will hear air hissing as it escapes along the side of the cork. It should then hold fast inside the neck of the bottle.

Finally, wipe bottles clean, label and store.

Plastic stoppers and caps do not fit as tightly as straight sided corks or cork stoppers and occasionally fly off in hot weather after heat expansion.

You can keep them in place by fitting a sheet of polythene cut into a 4 inch (102mm) square; smoothed over the top of

the bottle and fastened around the neck with two elastic
bands, string or strong thread. Two elastic bands are used in
case one perishes and snaps. Any that do still rise a fraction
can be pushed back when you notice them. Chemical-free
wines ought to have their corks (of whatever type) covered as
described as a matter of course, because of the unlikely but
possible danger of any secondary fermentation referred to
on pages 58 and 59.

If a small amount of wine is left after bottling you may:

a) Drink it.
b) Pour it into a bottle set aside for cooking wine. Keep two
   – one for red and one for white.
c) Use it while it is fresh and hasn't turned at all vinegary for
   topping up fermenting or maturing wine of similar
   flavour and colour.

18
Smarten Your Bottles

Present your wine in the bottle so it looks smart, clean and pleases the eye.

The bottle should offer a tantalizing invitation to sample its contents. With this in mind some wine makers prefer to brush off dust and cobwebs before offering it to guests.

Bottles look better labelled and capped.

You can buy printed labels displaying many beautiful designs, ready gummed or ungummed. Plastic and foil caps are also sold. No special device is needed to put them in place. Just push them down over the top of the bottle.

You can make your own caps from aluminium foil cut into 4 inch (102mm) squares, smoothed over the top of the bottle and trimmed neatly around the edge with scissors. Labels are fun designing and easily made. Felt-tip pens are useful for this.

You might choose to dedicate your finest wine to a special person or memorable occasion by writing on the label,

'Bottled With Love For ....

or

Bottled In Honour Of ....

You could write a loving message on a small piece of card; pierce a hole, loop some thread through and hang it round the bottle neck, so it rests on the shoulder.

Gift labels, bought from stationers and newsagents, look good used this way.

Labels can excite, be serious, or jolly and humorous and inject fun into the business of opening the bottle. The wine takes over where light hearted banter about its label ends.

You can devise and colour a crest and motto, or create imaginative names for wines. You might think Tea and Prune sounds more enticing to the uninitiated if you call it

Tepru Nectar. Once your guests taste it, are suitably impressed and hooked by the flavour, you may safely reveal the contents.

Glue or tape the label between the two seams of the bottle about 1½ inches (38mm) below the shoulder.

Do not use extra-strong glue, one day the label has to come off. An ordinary paper-glue serves well.

Attractively labelled, foil capped bottles of country wine, make most acceptable gifts and are an inexpensive but thoughtful way of saying 'thank you'.

If this seems a lot of fuss over what you regard as a plain bottle of hooch, then attach a simple label so you know which wine the bottle holds and when guests arrive, gently pour it into a decanter and serve from that.

Always include on the label a note of the date the wine was racked into a storage vessel, to give you an indication of how mature it is.

19
Serving Wine

Wine may be drunk and enjoyed by its maker at any stage of development but guests deserve some consideration. Wine should be bright and clear and matured to a smooth, vinous texture.

Country wines are unique in their superb range of colour and aroma and should be served in clear glasses to highlight their gloriously rich colours.

If an otherwise excellent wine shows a hint of haze in clear glass, it may be served in a goblet or decorated or tinted glass. This masks the slight imperfection.

Because wine continues developing and improving in the bottle, there is likely to be sediment. The raised punt at the base of wine bottles is designed to trap and hold sediment. Bear this in mind when pouring. Keep the bottle tilted at an angle, so sediment remains undisturbed. Decanting wine and serving from a decanter avoids this problem.

To sweeten wine
To sweeten a bottle of wine before serving, pour a cupful of the wine into a saucepan and heat until warm – not boiling. Add 1 level *table*spoon of granulated sugar, or 1 heaped *table*spoon of pure honey of your choice, or 1 level *table*spoon of concentrated wine making grape juice (red or white depending on the colour of your wine). Stir until dissolved. Cover and allow to cool. Then pour the sweetened wine back into the bottle or a decanter. This action will itself be enough for blending to occur within a short while. You may increase or decrease the amount of sweetening to suit your taste or the preference of guests.

All wine, apart from sparkling wine, improves in quality and aroma or bouquet, if allowed to breathe before being served.

Expose country wine to air by removing the cork from the bottle or decanting it before an evening's entertaining. White wine benefits from two to three hours absorption of air and red wine from three to six hours.

White and sparkling wine tastes better chilled before serving and red wine is at its best if stood in a warm room for an hour or two before being tasted.

Glasses should not be more than two-thirds filled, leaving room at the top of the glass for the wine's impressive bouquet to form.

Always serve some food with wine to enhance its appeal and absorb alcohol. Remember, country wines are deceptively strong. Cheese and biscuits complement all wine and cheese cleans the palate, enabling you to enjoy sampling different types of wine and fully appreciate subtle variations in their blending and balance.

Keep dregs for topping up

Keep dregs left in bottles for cooking, or for topping up fermenting wine or wine racked into a storage vessel to mature.

Topping up fermenting wine is necessary to compensate for a reduction in liquid volume due to the wine yeast's conversion of natural sugar (fructose and glucose) and/or household sugar (sucrose) to alcohol. Maturing wine is topped up to replace sediment discarded after racking, see page 63. When topping up wine, use left over white wine for white wines and red wine for red wines.

Always check that the left over wine tastes all right before using it. If it tastes vinegary, reserve it for cooking, or throw it away.

20
Vinegar

Wine vinegar is expensive to buy and easy to make.

You may set out to make it or simply fully convert a wine infected by the vinegar fly (Drosophila Melanogaster).

Vinegar has many culinary uses. It adds to the appetizing appeal of fish and chips, is used for pickling, adds zest to salads and is an important ingredient in salad dressings, mayonnaise and sauces for cooking.

Wine Vinegar – Method
Choose any matured, clear wine which is ready for bottling. Dilute each pint (½ litre) of wine you wish to convert to vinegar with ½ pint (284ml) of water. Add ½ pint (284ml) of commercial vinegar – wine or malt vinegar – to each 1½ pints (852ml) of diluted wine.

Now half fill a sterilised, *rinsed* narrow-necked glass vessel with the mixture. *Polythene vessels are unsuitable because they absorb the taste and aroma of vinegar and cannot be satisfactorily cleansed of it.* Leave the vessel half full. Air must be allowed to reach the wine to aid its transformation into vinegar. Plug the top of your glass vessel with cotton wool.

Put it somewhere warm and leave for at least eight weeks.

The wine/vinegar becomes hazy and a wrinkled skin forms on the surface. When the process is complete the vinegar starts clearing.

Bottling vinegar
When the vinegar has cleared – then, in one operation: 1) Syphon into sterilised, *rinsed* wine bottles. Fill to within 2¼ inches (57mm) of the top of the bottle. 2) Lightly cork the bottles with sterilised, *rinsed* cork or plastic stoppers, or plug

with cotton wool. 3) Pasteurise the vinegar. Half fill a large saucepan with water. Heat until hot, but not boiling. Place a wooden board, thick cloth or folded newspaper in the water and stand the bottles on it – make sure they are steady.

Maintain the water temperature just off boiling for thirty minutes, then switch off heat and fasten sterilised, *rinsed* cork or polythene stoppers into the bottles.

Label and store. The vinegar is ready for use after three months.

Remember to keep vinegar well away from stocks of wine. There is a risk the aroma may taint them and if any vinegar comes into contact with them, they too will turn to vinegar.

Thoroughly clean and sterilise all equipment used.

21
Useful Things To Make

As your experience and skill develop you will see many ways an easily constructed gadget can assist you.

Here are three ideas to start with. You need a few tools such as a drill, saw, screwdriver, screws and glasspaper.

Masher
A wooden mallet for effectively mashing fruit for fermentation.

Simply, a block of hardwood and a suitable length of dowel rod fitted through a hole in the centre of the block and wedged into place.

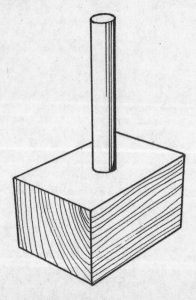

Masher.

Flogger

Essential aid for sinking straight sided corks into necks of bottles.

A strip of wood screwed to a hardwood block.

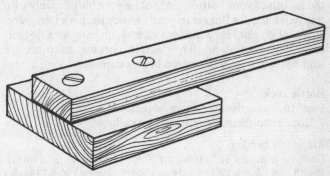

Flogger.

Using your flogger

Fill a bottle with wine to within 2¼ inches (57mm) of the top of the bottle. This allows room for the cork and leaves some

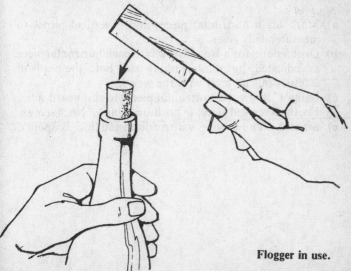

Flogger in use.

air space. Stand the wine-filled bottle upright on a hard surface. Press a straight sided cork, sterilised and softened by soaking for 24 hours in a sealed jar of sulphite solution (sodium metabisulphite mixed with water, see page 31) into the mouth of your bottle – and holding the bottle firmly with one hand, use the flogger to gently knock the cork into place.

If you do not fancy the idea of making your own flogger, hand held corkers and lever action corking machines are sold by shops stocking home brew equipment.

Bottle rack
Easy to make. Holds twelve bottles.
   Similar to those commercially available.

Materials needed
Beech – 6 pieces 16″ (406mm) × ¾″ (19mm) × ⅜″ (9mm)
Beech – 8 pieces 19¾″ (501mm) × ¾″ (19mm) × ⅜″ (9mm)
Chipboard – 2 pieces 16″ (406mm) × 7″ (178mm) × ½″ (13mm)
C.H. (Chipboard) Screws – 24 – ⅝″ No. 4
                                         – 16 – 1″ No. 4

Method
a) Mark off 8 horizontal pieces and 6 vertical pieces to measurements given.
b) Drill 5 holes for a No. 4 screw into each horizontal piece as indicated. By countersinking each hole, the heads of screws can sink level with the wood.
c) Using 1″ screws fix horizontal pieces to chipboard sides.
d) Fix the 6 vertical pieces in position using ⅝″ No. 4 screws.
e) Smooth off all surfaces with medium and fine glasspaper.

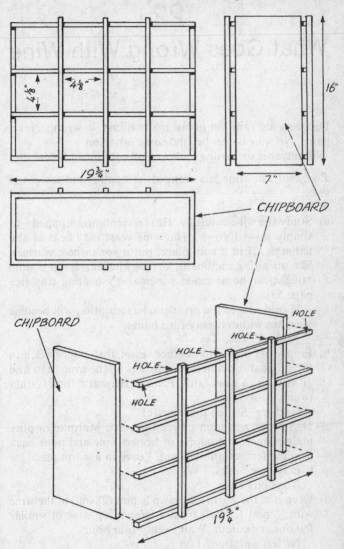

CHIPBOARD

CHIPBOARD

HOLE

HOLE

HOLE

HOLE

HOLE

22

What Goes Wrong With Wine

Disasters are rare but occasionally things go wrong. Never panic. No wine is ever beyond some salvation.

Remember to sterilise and *rinse* all equipment before use.

Problem: The wine has stopped fermenting but tastes too sweet.

Solution:

a) Study the wine carefully. Has fermentation stopped – or simply slowed down? The wine yeast may be cold and lethargic. If in a cool place, put it somewhere warmer, like an airing cupboard, or the kitchen, or on a shop bought, or home made winemaker's heating tray (see page 57).

   If cold caused the problem, fermentation will become vigorous within twenty-four hours.

   No luck? Then Try:

b) Empty the wine into another vessel, then pour back into the original container. This shakes up the wine yeast and gives it air to work with. Place in the warm for a further twenty-four hours.

   Nothing? Switch to action (c):

c) Dissolve ¼ *tea*spoon of yeast extract, Marmite or pure malt extract, in a cupful of heated wine and pour back into the fermentation vessel. Leave in a warm place for twenty-four hours.

   No good? Then:

d) Keep it in the warm and swap ½ pint (284ml) of the wine with ½ pint (284ml) from a fermenting wine of similar flavour and colour. Wait twenty-four hours.

   No fermentation? Try:

e) Exchange 1 pint (½ litre). If you do not have a fermenting wine, or (e) is not successful, attempt (f):

f) Pour the wine into an empty fermentation vessel. Take care not to disturb the bed of wine yeast at the bottom of the original container. Dissolve ¼ *tea*spoon of yeast extract, Marmite or pure malt extract, in 1 pint (½ litre) of warm water and add juice of a lemon or orange. Allow to cool and pour on to the wine yeast. This reactivates it. Leave for twenty-four hours, then add ½ pint (284ml) of the wine. After a further twenty-four hours add 1 pint (½ litre) of wine. Wait until it is fermenting well and add another pint (½ litre) and so on, until all the wine is working.

   Still nothing? Do not despair.

g) Put the wine to one side. It comes to no harm and is maturing and improving all the time. Make sure it is well covered. Wait until you make a wine of similar flavour and colour, too dry or sharp for your liking. When it has finished fermenting swap half of the too sweet wine with the dry (non-sweet) one. Both wines may ferment for a short while as active wine yeast present in the dry wine ferments residual natural sugar (fructose and glucose) and/or household sugar (sucrose) in the sweet wine. Both wines should settle down to become medium dry.

Problem: The fermenting wine has become thick in texture and appears to be setting, like jelly. It pours in long coils, but its taste is unaffected.

Solution: It looks unpleasant but is all right. Lactic acid bacteria have got to it. Pour the wine into a large saucepan, cover and boil. Maintain at the boil for five minutes to kill bacteria, then switch off heat and allow to cool. Begin fermentation with new yeast again (see page 54).

Problem: The fermenting wine smells of vinegar and has a bitter taste.

Solution: The vinegar fly has infected your wine. This problem is avoided when vessels are kept covered securely. You now have 1 gallon (4½ litres) of wine vinegar. Refer to the section on making vinegar on page 74 and complete the conversion.

Problem: The surface of the fermenting wine is covered by

flower-like chains of white powder.

Solution: The wine is infected by airborne bacteria and unless treated can turn eventually to little other than carbon dioxide and water.

Strain the wine through sterilised *rinsed* muslin and discard powdery substance. If necessary, repeat the process, but this time strain through a wad of cotton wool wedged into the bottom of a funnel.

Add the juice of a lemon or orange to kill bacteria, and continue fermentation.

Problem: The matured wine is ready for bottling, but tastes too sharp or tart.

Solution: Too much acid in the wine.

a) sweeten it by dissolving 3 level *table*spoons of household sugar (sucrose), or 3 heaped *table*spoons of pure honey, of your choice, or 3 fl oz (85ml) of concentrated wine making grape juice – red or white, the same colour as your country wine, per gallon (4½ litres) of wine, in a cupful of the warmed wine, returning it to the main bulk when cool. This balances the acidity.

b) If you prefer, mix it with a mature, ready for bottling, over-sweet wine of similar flavour and colour you have in stock. Allow two months for the wines to blend before bottling.

Problem: The matured wine is ready for bottling but lacks bite and tastes flat and lifeless.

Solution: Add 1 *table*spoon of strained, brewed tea per gallon (4½ litres) of wine to increase tannin level. Then bottle.

Problem: The matured wine is ready for bottling, but tastes too thin and watery.

Solution: Mix it with a full-bodied, mature, ready for bottling wine of similar flavour and colour. Allow two months for the wines to blend before bottling.

23
Sparkling Wine

Sparkling wine is romantic, refreshing and revitalizing. Any dry tasting (non-sweet) country wine matured for the minimum time suggested in the recipe and ready for bottling, can be given a sparkle, providing potassium sorbate was not added after the wine finished fermenting to inhibit wine yeast from further activity (see chapter 14).

The most popular sparkling country wines are apple, elderflower, gooseberry, peach, rose petal and strawberry.

Choose your favourite country wine and give it a sparkle.

It will be sparkling and ready to enjoy after 4 months in the bottle.

Do not cut corners with this prince among wines.

Use ONLY Champagne bottles.

They look best and are designed to withstand the high pressure of carbon dioxide gas in sparkling wine.

Other bottles may explode! Exploding bottles can cause serious injury. Never use cracked or chipped bottles.

Collect empty Champagne bottles from hotels, restaurants and wine bars. Ask nicely and staff are usually pleased to save them for you.

Some home brew shops sell used Champagne bottles.

To make six bottles of your favourite wine sparkle you need:

1 gallon (4½ litres) of the chosen, mature country wine – ready for bottling.

6 Champagne bottles.

6 Champagne-type stoppers.

6 Champagne wire hoods.

6 Champagne bottle foils.

6 Champagne labels.

5 fl oz (142ml) of pure, unsweetened grape juice – red or

white, the same colour as your country wine.
1 packet of dried Champagne yeast.

or

1 phial of liquid natural Champagne yeast.

Visit your local home brew stockist and buy Champagne-type stoppers, wire hoods to keep them firmly in place, stylish Champagne labels and Champagne bottle foils to decoratively cover the stoppers giving a final flourish to your bottles.

Having acquired your sparkling wine accessories, sterilise and *rinse* a good length of plastic syphon tube, an empty 1 gallon (4½ litres) narrow-necked fermentation vessel and a cork or rubber bung.

Put the storage vessel containing your chosen country wine on a surface at a higher level than the empty fermentation vessel; place the syphon tubing in the storage vessel just above any sediment, suck some wine into the tube and lower the other end into the empty fermentation vessel. Wine flows from the storage vessel into the fermentation vessel.

When full, fasten the cork or rubber bung in the neck of the fermentation vessel and set it aside.

Sterilise and rinse a bottle of 1 pint (½ litre) capacity.

Pour 5 fl oz (142ml) of pure, unsweetened grape juice – red or white, the same colour as your country wine, into the bottle.

WARNING – Never exceed the recommended measure of pure grape juice or your bottles may explode!

Add Champagne yeast to the bottle and plug with cotton wool, or cover with a 4 inch (102mm) square of sterilised, *rinsed* polythene, fastened securely with an elastic band, string or strong thread.

Keep it somewhere warm for 24 hours to begin fermenting.

After 24 hours pour a cupful of country wine from the fermentation vessel into a saucepan and heat until warm – not boiling. Add 2 level *table*spoons of granulated sugar, or 2 heaped *table*spoons of pure honey. Stir until dissolved. Cover and allow to cool.

WARNING – Never exceed the recommended measure

of granulated sugar, or pure honey or your bottles may explode!

Remove 5 fl oz (142ml) of country wine from the narrow-necked fermentation vessel and bottle it for drinking, cooking or topping up fermenting or maturing wines. Now you can pour the 5 fl oz (142ml) of fermenting pure grape juice into the fermentation vessel. Add the cool, sweetened wine from your saucepan and plug the fermentation vessel with cotton wool, or cover it with a 7 inch (178mm) square of sterilised, *rinsed* polythene, smoothed over the top of the fermentation vessel and secured around the neck with an elastic band, string or strong thread.

Keep the fermentation vessel in a warm place for 24 hours.

After 24 hours all the wine should be fermenting. You can check, if you like, by attaching an air lock, filled with water, to a bored cork or rubber bung fitted into the neck of the fermentation vessel. Bubbles of carbon dioxide gas should pass slowly, but regularly, up through the water.

Sterilise and rinse your syphon tubing, Champagne bottles and stoppers.

Soak cork stoppers in a sealed jar filled with sulphite solution (sodium metabisulphite mixed with water, see page 31) for thirty minutes.

Syphon the wine into the bottles to within 2¼ inches (57mm) of the top of each bottle; fasten stoppers, attach wire hoods and twist tight. Wipe bottles and smooth bottle foil over stoppers and wire hoods. Label and keep somewhere cool for at least 4 months before drinking.

Always stand bottles of sparkling wine upright.

Chill before serving.

When opening, cover the bottle with a clean cloth to catch the stopper.

Never shake the bottle.

Never hold it near your face.

Point it away from guests.

Pour carefully. Because the wine has fermented in bottle, there is sediment at the bottom.

24
Liqueurs

Nothing matches the splendid luxury of an after dinner liqueur. In traditional country liqueur recipes fruit is marinated in brandy or gin and a suggested method follows at the end of this chapter. In addition any matured, ready to drink bottle of country wine can be transformed into a rich liqueur with the assistance of a few extras.

With these converted country wines which we look at first, your bottle of country liqueur is ready to enjoy in 1 month. The alcohol content will be about 20% alcohol per volume (35% proof).

The ingredients required to make 1 standard size wine bottle of liqueur are:

17 fl oz (483ml) of matured, ready to drink country wine, of your choice.

7 fl oz (199ml) of Vodka – 37.5% alcohol per volume (65.5% proof).

Liqueur flavouring, a few drops – to your taste.

6 level *table*spoons of granulated sugar

or

6 heaped *table*spoons of pure honey, of your choice.

Liqueur flavourings

At the time of writing, over thirty different liqueur flavourings are marketed. Visit your home brew stockist and marvel at the choice.

A few drops of one of these inexpensive flavourings gives your wine a liqueur-like taste, similar to its expensive commercial equivalent.

Flavourings are formulated to reproduce the essence of liqueurs ranging from Campari, Cointreau, Crème de Menthe and Green Chartreuse to Italian Strega, Plum

Brandy, Rum, and Tia Maria. Your friendly home brew stockist will be pleased to guide your choice of flavouring.

Unique, tasty liqueurs can be produced using any combination of country wine and liqueur flavouring but your liqueur is more authentic if you use a wine made from ingredients similar to those employed in making the commercial liqueur.

For instance:

Country wine		Liqueur flavouring
Apricot wine	for	Apricot liqueur
Cherry wine	for	Cherry Brandy
Peach wine	for	Cusinier
Peppermint wine	for	Crème de Menthe
Plum wine	for	Plum Brandy
Sloe wine	for	Pedlar
	etc.	

Method
Heat a cupful of mature, ready to drink, country wine in a saucepan until warm – not boiling. Add 6 level *table*spoons of granulated sugar, or 6 heaped *table*spoons of pure honey. Stir until dissolved. Then cover and allow to cool.

Sterilise and rinse an empty wine bottle, polythene funnel and a cork or plastic stopper. Place the funnel in the neck of the empty wine bottle and pour the vodka and the cool, sweetened wine from the saucepan into the bottle. Then fill with country wine to within 3 inches (76mm) of the top of the bottle. Add several drops of liqueur flavouring. Fit the stopper in the bottle and wait 2 minutes for the flavouring to spread through the wine. Then pour some of the wine/liqueur into a glass and sip. Do not be put off by the confused mixture of tastes – they quickly smooth and blend.

Decide whether you wish to add a few more drops of liqueur flavouring. You can use up to ½ fl oz (14ml).

When satisfied with the balance of taste, top up with country wine to within 2¼ inches (57mm) of the top of the bottle. Then fasten the stopper.

Store for 1 month before drinking.

Serve liqueurs at room temperature in liqueur glasses.

Traditional country liqueurs

For liqueurs made the traditional country way any fresh fruit can be used. Your bottle of traditional country liqueur is ready to enjoy in 3 months. The alcohol content will be about 40% alcohol per volume (70% proof).

To make 1 standard size wine bottle of liqueur you need:
1 pint (½ litre) of brandy or gin.
1 lb (½kg) of fresh fruit, of your choice.
8 oz (227gm) of granulated sugar
   or
9 oz (255gm) of pure honey, of your choice.
1 screw top jar, big enough to hold all the ingredients.

Favourite fruit
Apricot (brandy), blackberry (gin), blackcurrant (gin), cherry (brandy), peach (brandy), raspberry (brandy), sloe (gin), and strawberry (brandy).

Method
Wash fresh fruit, of your choice, in cold water. Remove and discard cores, stalks and stones. Thinly slice large fruit; prick berries with a needle. Place fruit in the sterilised, *rinsed* jar. Add granulated sugar or pure honey and pour in brandy or gin. Fill jar to the top and screw lid tight. Store for 3 months. Stir daily until sugar or honey is dissolved.

The brandy or gin sterilises and preserves the fruit and extracts flavour and colour.

After 3 months strain through sterilised, *rinsed* muslin or scissor trimmed tights into a sterilised, *rinsed* wine or liqueur bottle and fasten a sterilised, *rinsed* cork or plastic stopper.

The liqueur is ready immediately for drinking.

Eat the delicious fruit.

25
Notes On Recipes

Each recipe details ingredients and method for making excellent, economical country wine AND superb natural, sugar-free country wine. The recipes are also designed for wine production *free* of chemical additives. Since the many wine-makers who do use additives to save time and worry regard them as harmless, full consideration of their advantages is given in chapter 11. The correct times to add them are shown in chapters 14 and 17.

The method of preparing ingredients for recipes in this book is the same irrespective of the type of wine being made. It may be successfully applied to the making of any wine.

Cold water extraction of flavour and colour is favoured because boiling and scalding destroys valuable oils and scents and releases pectin which clouds wine, inhibiting its clearing.

Recipes are for 1 gallon (4½ litres) of wine. If you wish to make your wine in larger or smaller quantities, adjust the measure of ingredients accordingly.

Each recipe uses raisins (dried black grapes) or sultanas (dried white grapes) to provide nutrient and body to nourish the wine yeast and encourage its efficiency and effectiveness.

Raisins and sultanas also add flavour, colour and a silky, smooth, vinosity to the finished wine and they speed its maturing, making it ready for drinking sooner.

At the start of stage 1 fermentation, leave space at the top of your bucket or bin for frothing and foaming; 2″ (51mm)–4″ (102mm), is a suggested minimum, or you may find fermenting wine spilling on to the floor. The wider your bucket or bin, the less room you need leave.

Whether fermentation stage 2 will take 4-5 weeks as per the recipes, or whether there may be minor variations will

depend how reasonably close to 18°C (64°F) you are able
to maintain an even temperature.

A suggested minimum period for maturing wine before
drinking is given for each recipe. This is intended as an
approximate guide; much depends on your personal taste.

Flavour and quality can improve dramatically – sometimes over weeks, sometimes months and sometimes years,
and country wine should be given an opportunity appropri-
ate to its type to mature fully before being enjoyed.

Each recipe gives an indication of when you can expect
your wine to reach peak perfection. As mentioned on
page 33 wine matures better in bulk, so do not bottle too
early.

26
Quick Index
To Principles And Methods

Bottling	66
Chemical-free wines	46
Clearing	64

Fermentation:

Wine yeast starter bottle	53
Stage 1	55
Covering buckets and bins	56
Racking after stage 1	61
Stage 2	56
Covering fermentation vessel	56
Judging when fermentation finished	58
Racking after stage 2	62
Secondary fermentation	59

Records	42
Safety and cleanliness	29
Sparkling wines	83
Sterilising equipment	31
Storage	32
Storage vessels	33
Sugar-free wines	49
Sulphite solution	31
Sweetening wine	71
What goes wrong	80

27
Recipes For Cheats

You may not want to wait several months or a year before opening your country wine. Resist the temptation to break into your store of maturing country wines.

If you must cheat there are wines you can make which, though not as excellent as country wines, will be ready for drinking shortly after they have finished fermenting. Drink these and spare your improving country wines until fully matured.

'Cheat' wines are made the same way as country wines, except pure natural juices are bought and poured straight into your bucket or wide-mouthed container. To encourage quick maturing no tannin or acid is added.

These wines are soon ready for drinking, do not improve significantly beyond a year and are not suitable for long term storage.

Pure, natural juices, bought from your health food stockist, are essential. Artificially sweetened, chemically clogged juices will not ferment satisfactorily.

All recipes are for 1 gallon (4½ litres) of wine.

Pure Apple Juice

'Cheat' Wine

Delightful light table wine. Ready to drink 10 weeks after the fermented wine has been transferred to a storage vessel to clear and mature.

Alcohol content about 9.5% alcohol per volume (17% proof).

Use only pure apple juice bought from your health food stockist.

Sultanas (dried white grapes) give extra flavour, body and smoothness to this wine and nourish the wine yeast, encouraging maximum efficiency in alcohol production.

Ingredients: To make 1 gallon (4½ litres)

Country recipe
Pure apple juice – 1¾ pints (1 litre)
Sultanas – 4 oz (113gm)
Granulated sugar – 1½ lbs (680gm)

Natural, sugar-free recipe
Pure apple juice – 1¾ pints (1 litre)
Sultanas – 8 oz (227gm)
Pure acacia blossom honey – 12 oz (340gm)
Pure white grape juice – 1¾ pints (1 litre)
or
Concentrated wine making white grape juice – ½ pint (284ml)

Both recipes
Yeast extract – ¼ teaspoon, or Marmite – ¼ teaspoon, or pure malt extract – ¼ teaspoon
and
All-purpose wine yeast starter bottle or all-purpose dried wine yeast or all-purpose liquid natural wine

Pure Apple Juice—contd.

yeast
and
Water to 1 gallon (4½ litres)

Method – Stage 1

Pour pure apple juice into bucket. Add sultanas after rinsing in warm water and chopping or mincing. Cover. Warm 1 pint (½ litre) of water in large saucepan. Stir in granulated sugar, or pure honey and yeast extract, or Marmite, or pure malt extract. When dissolved, cover and allow to cool. Then pour into bucket. For sugar-free recipe, add pure grape juice or concentrated grape juice. Both recipes – add ¾ of wine yeast starter bottle, or the quantity directed by the supplier of the dried wine yeast, or liquid natural wine yeast. Top up to 7 pints (4 litres) with cold water. Allow at least 2" (51mm)–4" (102mm) at the top of your bucket for frothing and foaming. Cover. Leave in a warm place for 10 days. Stir twice daily.

Method – Stage 2

After 10 days rack the fermenting wine from its sediment and strain into a narrow-necked 1 gallon (4½ litres) fermentation vessel. Discard solids. Top up to the neck with cold water. Cover. Leave to ferment to dryness. This can take 4–5 weeks at an even temperature of 18°C (64°F).

Wait 2 weeks after fermentation has finished; then rack wine from its sediment into a narrow-necked 1 gallon (4½ litres) storage vessel. Top up to the neck with wine of similar flavour and colour, or cold water. Fit a cork or rubber bung and keep somewhere cool for 10 weeks to clear and mature.

After 10 weeks' storage the wine should be clear and ready for bottling, though you can leave it longer.

When bottled, your apple 'cheat' wine is ready for drinking.

It achieves peak perfection about 10 months after being racked into a storage vessel to clear and mature.

Pure Blackcurrant Juice

'Cheat' Wine

Delicious. Ready to drink 9 weeks after the fermented wine has been transferred to a storage vessel to clear and mature.

Alcohol content about 9.5% alcohol per volume (17% proof).

Use only pure blackcurrant juice bought from your health food stockist.

Raisins (dried black grapes) give extra flavour, body and smoothness to this wine and nourish wine yeast, encouraging maximum efficiency in alcohol production.

Ingredients: To make 1 gallon (4½ litres)

Country recipe
Pure blackcurrant juice –
  1¾ pints (1 litre)
Raisins – 4 oz (113gm)
Granulated sugar – 1½ lbs
  (680gm)

Natural, sugar-free recipe
Pure blackcurrant juice –
  1¾ pints (1 litre)
Raisins – 8 oz (227 gm)
Pure orange blossom honey
  – 12 oz (340 gm)
Pure red grape juice – 1¾
  pints (1 litre)
or
Concentrated wine making
  red grape juice – ½ pint
  (284ml)

Both recipes
Yeast extract – ¼
teaspoon, or Marmite – ¼
teaspoon, or pure malt
extract – ¼ teaspoon
and
All-purpose wine yeast
starter bottle or all-purpose
dried wine yeast or all-
purpose liquid natural wine

Pure Blackcurrant Juice—contd.
yeast
and
Water to 1 gallon (4½ litres)

Method – Stage 1

Pour pure blackcurrant juice into bucket. Add raisins after rinsing in warm water and chopping or mincing. Cover. Warm 1 pint (½ litre) of water in large saucepan. Stir in granulated sugar, or pure honey and yeast extract, or Marmite, or pure malt extract. When dissolved, cover and allow to cool. Then pour into bucket. For sugar-free recipe, add pure grape juice or concentrated grape juice. Both recipes – add ¾ of wine yeast starter bottle, or the quantity directed by the supplier of the dried wine yeast, or liquid natural wine yeast. Top up to 7 pints (4 litres) with cold water. Allow at least 2″ (51mm)–4 inches (102mm) at the top of your bucket for frothing and foaming. Cover. Leave in a warm place for 10 days. Stir twice daily.

Method – Stage 2

After 10 days rack the fermenting wine from its sediment and strain into a narrow-necked 1 gallon (4½ litres) fermentation vessel. Discard solids. Top up to the neck with cold water. Cover. Leave to ferment to dryness. This can take 4–5 weeks at an even temperature of 18°C (64°F).

Wait 2 weeks after fermentation has finished; then rack wine from its sediment into a narrow-necked 1 gallon (4½ litres) storage vessel. Top up to the neck with wine of similar flavour and colour, or cold water. Fit a cork or rubber bung and keep somewhere cool for 9 weeks to clear and mature.

After 9 weeks' storage the wine should be clear and ready for bottling. Leave it longer if you prefer.

When bottled, your blackcurrant 'cheat' wine is ready for drinking.

It achieves peak perfection about 11 months after being racked into a storage vessel to clear and mature.

Pure Apple And Blackcurrant Juice

'Cheat' Wine

Nectar. Ready to drink 10 weeks after the fermented wine has been transferred to a storage vessel to clear and mature.

Alcohol content about 12% alcohol per volume (21% proof).

Use only pure apple and blackcurrant juice bought from your health food stockist.

Sultanas (dried white grapes) give extra flavour, body and smoothness to this wine and nourish wine yeast, encouraging maximum efficiency in alcohol production.

Ingredients: To make 1 gallon (4½ litres)

Country recipe
Pure apple juice – 1 pint (½ litre)
Pure blackcurrant juice – 1 pint (½ litre)
Sultanas – 4 oz (113gm)
Granulated sugar – 2 lbs (907gm)

Natural, sugar-free recipe
Pure apple juice – 1 pint (½ litre)
Pure blackcurrant juice – 1 pint (½ litre)
Sultanas – 8 oz (227gm)
Pure lime blossom honey – 1 lb (454gm)
Pure white grape juice – 3½ pints (2 litres)
or
Concentrated wine making white grape juice – 1 pint (½ litre)

Both recipes
Yeast extract – ¼ teaspoon, or Marmite – ¼ teaspoon, or pure malt extract – ¼ teaspoon and
All-purpose wine yeast starter bottle or all-purpose dried wine yeast or all-purpose liquid natural wine

Pure Apple And Blackcurrant Juice—contd.

yeast
and
Water to 1 gallon (4½
litres)

Method – Stage 1

Pour pure apple and blackcurrant juice into bucket. Add
sultanas after rinsing in warm water and chopping or
mincing. Cover. Warm 1 pint (½ litre) of water in large
saucepan. Stir in granulated sugar, or pure honey and yeast
extract, or Marmite, or pure malt extract. When dissolved,
cover and allow to cool. Then pour into bucket. For sugar-
free recipe, add pure grape juice or concentrated grape juice.
Both recipes – add ¾ of wine yeast starter bottle, or the
quantity directed by the supplier of the dried wine yeast, or
liquid natural wine yeast. Top up to 7 pints (4 litres) with
cold water. Allow at least 2″ (51mm)–4 inches (102mm) at
the top of your bucket for frothing and foaming. Cover.
Leave in a warm place for 10 days. Stir twice daily.

Method – Stage 2

After 10 days rack the fermenting wine from its sediment and
strain into a narrow-necked 1 gallon (4½ litres) fermentation
vessel. Discard solids. Top up to the neck with cold water.
Cover. Leave to ferment to dryness. This can take 4–5 weeks
at an even temperature of 18°C (64°F).

Wait 2 weeks after fermentation has finished; then rack
wine from its sediment into a narrow-necked 1 gallon (4½
litres) storage vessel. Top up to the neck with wine of similar
flavour and colour, or cold water. Fit a cork or rubber bung
and keep somewhere cool for 10 weeks to clear and mature.

After 10 weeks' storage the wine should be clear and ready
for bottling though it can be left longer.

When bottled, your apple and blackcurrant 'cheat' wine is
ready for drinking.

It achieves peak perfection about 11 months after being
racked into a storage vessel to clear and mature.

Pure Grapefruit Juice

'Cheat' Wine

Pleasant table wine. Ready to drink 12 weeks after the fermented wine has been transferred to a storage vessel to clear and mature.

Alcohol content about 10% alcohol per volume (17.5% proof).

Use only pure grapefruit juice bought from your health food stockist.

Sultanas (dried white grapes) give extra flavour, body and smoothness to this wine and nourish the wine yeast, encouraging maximum efficiency in alcohol production.

Ingredients: To make 1 gallon (4½ litres)

Country recipe
Pure grapefruit juice - 1 pint (½ litre)
Sultanas - 4 oz (113gm)
Granulated sugar - 2 lbs (907gm)

Natural, sugar-free recipe
Pure grapefruit juice - 1 pint (½ litre)
Sultanas - 8 oz (227gm)
Pure acacia blossom honey - 1 lb (454gm)
Pure white grape juice - 3½ pints (2 litres)
or
Concentrated wine making white grape juice - 1 pint (½ litre)

Both recipes
Yeast extract - ¼ teaspoon, or Marmite - ¼ teaspoon, or pure malt extract - ¼ teaspoon
and
All-purpose wine yeast starter bottle or all-purpose dried wine yeast or all-purpose liquid natural wine

Pure Grapefruit Juice—contd.

yeast
and
**Water to 1 gallon (4½
litres)**

Method – Stage 1

Pour pure grapefruit juice into bucket. Add sultanas after
rinsing in warm water and chopping or mincing. Cover.
Warm 1 pint (½ litre) of water in large saucepan. Stir in
granulated sugar, or pure honey and yeast extract, or
Marmite, or pure malt extract. When dissolved, cover and
allow to cool. Then pour into bucket. For sugar-free recipe,
add pure grape juice or concentrated grape juice. Both
recipes – add ¾ of wine yeast starter bottle, or the quantity
directed by the supplier of the dried wine yeast, or liquid
natural wine yeast. Top up to 7 pints (4 litres) with cold
water. Allow at least 2″ (51mm)–4 inches (102mm) at the top
of your bucket for frothing and foaming. Cover. Leave in a
warm place for 10 days. Stir twice daily.

Method – Stage 2

After 10 days rack the fermenting wine from its sediment and
strain into a narrow-necked 1 gallon (4½ litres) fermentation
vessel. Discard solids. Top up to the neck with cold water.
Cover. Leave to ferment to dryness. This can take 4–5 weeks
at an even temperature of 18°C (64°F).

Wait 2 weeks after fermentation has finished; then rack
wine from its sediment into a narrow-necked 1 gallon (4½
litres) storage vessel. Top up to the neck with wine of similar
flavour and colour, or cold water. Fit a cork or rubber bung
and keep somewhere cool for 12 weeks to clear and mature.

After 12 weeks' storage the wine should be clear and ready
for bottling. Leave longer if preferred.

When bottled, your grapefruit 'cheat' wine is ready for
drinking.

It achieves peak perfection about 11 months after being
racked into a storage vessel to clear and mature.

Pure Orange Juice

'Cheat' Wine

Full-flavoured wine. Ready to drink 12 weeks after the fermented wine has been transferred to a storage vessel to clear and mature.

Alcohol content about 10.5% alcohol per volume (18% proof).

Use only pure orange juice bought from your health food stockist.

Sultanas (dried white grapes) give extra flavour, body and smoothness to this wine and nourish wine yeast, encouraging maximum efficiency in alcohol production.

Ingredients: To make 1 gallon (4½ litres)

Country recipe
Pure orange juice – 1¾ pints (1 litre)
Sultanas – 4 oz (113gm)
Granulated sugar – 1¾ lbs (794gm)

Natural, sugar-free recipe
Pure orange juice – 1¾ pints (1 litre)
Sultanas – 8 oz (227gm)
Pure orange blossom honey – 1lb (454gm)
Pure white grape juice – 1¾ pints (1 litre)
or
Concentrated wine making white grape juice – ½ pint (284ml)

Both recipes
Yeast extract – ¼ teaspoon, or Marmite – ¼ teaspoon, or pure malt extract – ¼ teaspoon
and
All-purpose wine yeast starter bottle or all-purpose dried wine yeast or all-purpose liquid natural wine

Pure Orange Juice—contd.

**yeast
and
Water to 1 gallon (4½
litres)**

Method – Stage 1

Pour pure orange juice into bucket. Add sultanas after
rinsing in warm water and chopping or mincing. Cover.
Warm 1 pint (½ litre) of water in large saucepan. Stir in
granulated sugar, or pure honey and yeast extract, or
Marmite, or pure malt extract. When dissolved, cover and
allow to cool. Then pour into bucket. For sugar-free recipe,
add pure grape juice or concentrated grape juice. Both
recipes – add ¾ of wine yeast starter bottle, or the quantity
directed by the supplier of dried wine yeast, or liquid natural
wine yeast. Top up to 7 pints (4 litres) with cold water. Allow
at least 2″ (51mm)–4 inches (102mm) at the top of your
bucket for frothing and foaming. Cover. Leave in a warm
place for 10 days. Stir twice daily.

Method – Stage 2

After 10 days rack the fermenting wine from its sediment and
strain into a narrow-necked 1 gallon (4½ litres) fermentation
vessel. Discard solids. Top up to the neck with cold water.
Cover. Leave to ferment to dryness. This can take 4–5 weeks
at an even temperature of 18°C (64°F).

Wait 2 weeks after fermentation has finished; then rack
wine from its sediment into a narrow-necked 1 gallon (4½
litres) storage vessel. Top up to the neck with wine of similar
flavour and colour, or cold water. Fit a cork or rubber bung
and keep somewhere cool for 12 weeks to clear and mature.

After 12 weeks' storage the wine should be clear and ready
for bottling though you may wish to leave it for longer.

When bottled, your orange 'cheat' wine is ready for
drinking.

It achieves peak perfection about 11 months after being
racked into a storage vessel to clear and mature.

Pure Pineapple Juice

'Cheat' Wine

Fruity, appealing wine. Ready to drink 12 weeks after the fermented wine has been transferred to a storage vessel to clear and mature.

Alcohol content about 9.5% alcohol per volume (17% proof).

Use only pure pineapple juice bought from your health food stockist.

Sultanas (dried white grapes) give extra flavour, body and smoothness to this wine and nourish wine yeast, encouraging maximum efficiency in alcohol production.

Ingredients: To make 1 gallon (4½ litres)

Country recipe
Pure pineapple juice –
1¾ pints (1 litre)
Sultanas – 4 oz (113gm)
Granulated sugar – 1½ lbs
(680gm)

Natural, sugar-free recipe
Pure pineapple juice –
1¾ pints (1 litre)
Sultanas – 8 oz (227gm)
Pure lime blossom honey –
12 oz (340gm)
Pure white grape juice –
1¾ pints (1 litre)
or
Concentrated wine making
white grape juice – ½ pint
(284ml)

Both recipes
Yeast extract – ¼ teaspoon,
or Marmite – ¼ teaspoon, or
pure malt extract –
¼ teaspoon
and
All-purpose wine yeast
starter bottle or all-purpose
dried wine yeast or all-
purpose liquid natural wine

Pure Pineapple Juice—contd.

yeast
and
Water to 1 gallon (4½ litres)

Method - Stage 1

Pour pure pineapple juice into bucket. Add sultanas after rinsing in warm water and chopping or mincing. Cover. Warm 1 pint (½ litre) of water in large saucepan. Stir in granulated sugar, or pure honey and yeast extract, or Marmite, or pure malt extract. When dissolved, cover and allow to cool. Then pour into bucket. For sugar-free recipe, add pure grape juice or concentrated grape juice. Both recipes - add ¾ of wine yeast starter bottle, or the quantity directed by the supplier of dried wine yeast, or liquid natural wine yeast. Top up to 7 pints (4 litres) with cold water. Allow at least 2" (51mm)–4 inches (102mm) at the top of your bucket for frothing and foaming. Cover. Leave in a warm place for 10 days. Stir twice daily.

Method   Stage 2

After 10 days rack the fermenting wine from its sediment and strain into a narrow-necked 1 gallon (4½ litres) fermentation vessel. Discard solids. Top up to the neck with cold water. Cover. Leave to ferment to dryness. This can take 4–5 weeks at an even temperature of 18°C (64°F).

Wait 2 weeks after fermentation has finished; then rack wine from its sediment into a narrow-necked 1 gallon (4½ litres) storage vessel. Top up to the neck with wine of similar flavour and colour, or cold water. Fit a cork or rubber bung and keep somewhere cool for 12 weeks to clear and mature.

After 12 weeks' storage the wine should be clear and ready for bottling though you may wish to leave it for longer.

When bottled, your pineapple 'cheat' wine is ready for drinking.

It achieves peak perfection about 11 months after being racked into a storage vessel to clear and mature.

28
Wine Planner

To help spread your wine making over the year, here are month by month suggestions. Of course, you may make wines whenever ingredients are available.

JANUARY — Barley/Beetroot/Blackcurrant juice 'cheat'/Ginger/Parsnip/Rice and Raisin.

FEBRUARY — Beetroot/Grapefruit juice 'cheat'/Parsnip/Tea and Prune.

MARCH — Apple juice 'cheat'/Coltsfoot/Dandelion/Parsnip.

APRIL — Apple and Blackcurrant juice 'cheat'/Coltsfoot/Dandelion/Mead/Oak leaf.

MAY — Dandelion/Elderflower/Hawthorn blossom/Nettle/Oak leaf.

JUNE — Cherry/Dandelion/Elderflower/Gooseberry/Hawthorn blossom/Parsley/Rose petal.

JULY — Agrimony/Apricot/Blackcurrant/Cherry/Dandelion/Gooseberry/Hop/Parsley/Raspberry/Rose petal/Strawberry.

AUGUST — Agrimony/Apricot/Blackcurrant/Carrot/Cherry/Hop/Peach/Peppermint/Plum/Raspberry/Rose petal/Strawberry.

SEPTEMBER — Apple/Blackberry/Blackcurrant/Dandelion/Peach/Peppermint/Plum.

OCTOBER — Apple/Beetroot/Blackberry/Carrot/Elderberry/Rosehip/Sloe.

NOVEMBER — Apple/Beetroot/Carrot/Celery/

Elderberry/Pineapple juice 'cheat'/
Rosehip/Sloe.

DECEMBER   —   Beetroot/Carrot/Celery/Christmas
punch/Orange juice 'cheat'/Parsnip.

29
Recipes for Country Wines

Agrimony

Bracing, satisfying wine. Ready to drink 10 months after the fermented wine has been transferred to a storage vessel to clear and mature.

Alcohol content about 11.5% alcohol per volume (20% proof).

Sultanas (dried white grapes) give extra flavour, body and smoothness to this wine and nourish the wine yeast, encouraging maximum efficiency in alcohol production.

Ingredients: To make 1 gallon (4½ litres)

Country recipe
Agrimony leaves – 1¾ pints
 (1 litre)
or dried – 2 oz (56gm)
Sultanas – 8 oz (227gm)
Granulated sugar – 2 lbs
 (907gm)
Tea, strong – ½ cup
Oranges – 2

Natural, sugar-free recipe
Agrimony leaves –1¾ pints
 (1 litre)
or dried – 2 oz (56gm)
Sultanas – 12 oz (340gm)
Pure orange blossom honey
 – 1 lb (454gm)
Pure white grape juice –
 3½ pints (2 litres)
or
Concentrated wine making
 white grape juice – 1 pint
 (½ litre)
Tea, strong – ½ cup
Orange – 1

Both recipes
Yeast extract – ¼ teaspoon, or Marmite – ¼ teaspoon, or pure malt extract – ¼ teaspoon
and
All-purpose wine yeast starter bottle or all-purpose dried wine yeast or all-purpose liquid natural wine yeast
and
Water to 1 gallon (4½ litres)

Method – Stage 1

To measure fresh agrimony leaves, discard pieces of stalk and gently press leaves in measuring jug. Lightly rinse fresh leaves in cold water. Put fresh or dried leaves in bucket. Add sultanas after rinsing in warm water and chopping or mincing. Cover. Warm 1 pint (½ litre) of water in large saucepan. Stir in granulated sugar, or pure honey and yeast extract, or Marmite, or pure malt extract. When dissolved, cover and allow to cool. Then pour into bucket. For sugar-free recipe, add pure grape juice or concentrated grape juice. Cover. Both recipes – make tea, strain and allow to cool, or use strained cold tea from an earlier brew. Discard leaves or bag. Extract juice from orange. Discard pips, pith and peel. Place ingredients in bucket and add ¾ of wine yeast starter bottle, or the quantity directed by the supplier of the dried wine yeast, or liquid natural wine yeast. Top up to 7 pints (4 litres) with cold water. Allow at least 2" (51mm) -4 inches (102mm) at the top of your bucket for frothing and foaming. Cover. Leave in a warm place for 10 days. Stir twice daily.

Method – Stage 2

After 10 days rack the fermenting wine from its sediment and strain into a narrow-necked 1 gallon (4½ litre) fermentation vessel. Discard solids. Top up to the neck with cold water. Cover. Leave to ferment to dryness. This can take 4 5 weeks at an even temperature of 18°C (64°F).

Wait 2 weeks after fermentation has finished; then rack wine from its sediment into a narrow-necked 1 gallon (4½ litres) storage vessel. Top up to the neck with wine of similar flavour and colour, or cold water. Fit a cork or rubber bung and keep somewhere cool for 8 months to clear and mature.

After 8 months' storage the wine should be clear and ready for bottling.

When bottled, your agrimony wine needs a further 2–3 months to condition and mature before drinking.

It achieves peak perfection about 20 months after being racked into a storage vessel to clear and mature if you can bear to leave it in storage that long.

Apple

Fresh, light table wine. Any type of apple, or combination of varieties may be used. Ready to drink 11 months after the fermented wine has been transferred to a storage vessel to clear and mature.

*Apples make a particularly pleasant sparkling wine, see page 83.

Alcohol content about 11% alcohol per volume (19% proof).

Sultanas (dried white grapes) give extra flavour, body and smoothness to this wine and nourish the wine yeast, encouraging maximum efficiency in alcohol production.

Ingredients: To make 1 gallon (4½ litres)

Country recipe
Apples – 9 lbs (4Kg)
Sultanas – 12 oz (340gm)
Granulated sugar – 1¼ lbs (567gm)
Tea, strong – ½ cup
Lemons – 2

Natural, sugar-free recipe
Apples – 9 lb (4Kg)
Sultanas – 1 lb (454gm)
Pure acacia blossom honey – 12 oz (340gm)
Pure white grape juice – 1¾ pints (1 litre) or
Concentrated wine making white grape juice – ½ pint (284ml)
Tea, strong – ½ cup
Lemon – 1

Both recipes
Yeast extract – ¼ teaspoon,
or Marmite – ¼ teaspoon, or
pure malt extract –
¼ teaspoon
and
**All-purpose wine yeast
starter bottle or all-purpose
dried wine yeast or all-
purpose liquid natural wine
yeast
and
Water to 1 gallon (4½ litres)**

Method. – *Stage 1.*
Rinse apples in cold water. Cut into quarters; remove and
discard cores. Slice thinly, or mince apples (including skins)
and put them in bucket or bin keeping them under enough
water to prevent browning through contact with the air. (A
sterilized *rinsed* plate helps to hold them under the surface
and can remain throughout stage one). Add sultanas after
rinsing in warm water and chopping or mincing. Cover.
Warm 1 pint (½ litre) of water in large saucepan. Stir in
granulated sugar, or pure honey and yeast extract, or
Marmite, or pure malt extract. When dissolved, cover and
allow to cool. Then pour into bucket or bin. For sugar-free
recipe, add pure grape juice or concentrated grape juice.
Cover. Both recipes – make tea, strain and allow to cool,
discard leaves or bag. Extract juice only from lemon. Place
ingredients in bucket and add ¾ of wine yeast starter bottle, or
the quantity directed by the supplier of the dried wine yeast, or
liquid natural wine yeast. Top up to 7 pints (4 litres) with cold
water. Allow at least 2″ (51mm)–4 inches (102mm) at the top
of your bucket or bin for frothing and foaming. Cover bucket
or bin. Leave in a warm place for 10 days. Stir twice daily.

Method – Stage 2
After 10 days rack the fermenting wine from its sediment and
strain into a narrow-necked 1 gallon (4½ litres) fermentation
vessel. Discard solids. Top up to the neck with cold water.

Cover. Leave to ferment to dryness. This can take 4–5 weeks at an even temperature of 18°C (64°F).

Wait 2 weeks after fermentation has finished; then rack wine from its sediment into a narrow-necked 1 gallon (4½ litres) storage vessel. Top up to the neck with wine of similar flavour and colour, or cold water. Do NOT add potassium sorbate (see page 47) to your wine if you intend to make it sparkle. Fit a cork or rubber bung and keep somewhere cool for 9 months to clear and mature.

After 9 months' storage the wine should be clear and ready for bottling.

When bottled, your apple wine needs a further 2–3 months to condition and mature before drinking.

It achieves peak perfection about 24 months after being racked into a storage vessel to clear and mature if you can bear to leave it in storage that long.

Apricot

Most enjoyable wine. Warm, glowing colour. Ready to drink 10 months after the fermented wine has been transferred to a storage vessel to clear and mature.

Alcohol content about 13.5% alcohol per volume (24% proof).

Sultanas (dried white grapes) give extra flavour, body and smoothness to this wine and nourish the wine yeast, encouraging maximum efficiency in alcohol production.

Ingredients: To make 1 gallon (4½ litres)

Country recipe	*Natural, sugar-free recipe*
Apricots – 3¼ lbs (1½ Kg)	**Apricots – 3¼ lbs (1½ Kg)**
or dried – 10 oz (283gm)	**or dried – 10 oz (283gm)**
Sultanas – 12 oz (340gm)	**Sultanas – 1 lb (454gm)**
Granulated sugar – 2 lbs (907gm)	**Pure orange blossom honey – 1 lb (454gm)**
Tea, strong – ½ cup	**Pure white grape juice –**

Apricot—contd.

Oranges – 2

3½ pints (2 litres)
or
Concentrated wine making white grape juice – 1 pint (½ litre)
Tea, strong – ½ cup
Orange – 1

Both recipes
Yeast extract – ¼ teaspoon, or Marmite – ¼ teaspoon, or pure malt extract – ¼ teaspoon
and
All-purpose wine yeast starter bottle or all-purpose dried wine yeast or all-purpose liquid natural wine yeast
and
Water to 1 gallon (4½ litres)

Method – Stage 1

Cut fresh apricots in half and discard stones. Lightly rinse fresh apricots in cold water; then mash them in bucket. Rinse dried apricots in warm water; chop or mince and put in bucket. Add sultanas after rinsing in warm water and chopping or mincing. Cover. Warm 1 pint (½ litre) of water in large saucepan. Stir in granulated sugar, or pure honey and yeast extract, or Marmite, or pure malt extract. When dissolved, cover and allow to cool. Then pour into bucket. For sugar-free recipe, add pure grape juice or concentrated grape juice. Cover. Both recipes – make tea, strain and allow to cool, or use strained cold tea from an earlier brew. Discard leaves or bag. Extract juice from orange. Discard pips, pith and peel. Place ingredients in bucket and add ¾ of wine yeast starter bottle, or the quantity directed by the supplier of dried wine yeast, or liquid natural wine yeast. Top up to 7 pints (4 litres) with cold water. Allow at least 2″

(51mm)–4 inches (102mm) at the top of your bucket for frothing and foaming. Cover. Leave in a warm place for 10 days. Stir twice daily.

Method – Stage 2

After 10 days rack the fermenting wine from its sediment and strain into a narrow-necked 1 gallon (4½ litres) fermentation vessel. Discard solids. Top up to the neck with cold water. Cover. Leave to ferment to dryness. This can take 4–5 weeks at an even temperature of 18°C (64°F).

Wait 2 weeks after fermentation has finished; then rack wine from its sediment into a narrow-necked 1 gallon (4½ litres) storage vessel. Top up to the neck with wine of similar flavour and colour, or cold water. Fit a cork or rubber bung and keep somewhere cool for 8 months to clear and mature.

After 8 months' storage the wine should be clear and ready for bottling but a longer period can improve it.

When bottled, your apricot wine needs a further 2–3 months to condition and mature before drinking.

It achieves peak perfection about 24 months after being racked into a storage vessel to clear and mature.

Barley

Tasty, full bodied wine. Ready to drink 10 months after the fermented wine has been transferred to a storage vessel to clear and mature.

Alcohol content about 13% alcohol per volume (23% proof).

Raisins (dried black grapes) give extra flavour, body and smoothness to this wine and nourish the wine yeast, encouraging maximum efficiency in alcohol production.

Ingredients: To make 1 gallon (4½ litres)

Country recipe	*Natural, sugar-free recipe*
Pearl barley – 1½ lbs (680gm)	**Pearl barley – 1½ lb (680gm) or flaked barley – 1½ lbs**

Barley—contd.

or flaked barley – 1½ lbs
  (680gm)
Potatoes – 1 lb (454gm)
Raisins – 1 lb (454gm)
Granulated sugar – 2 lbs
  (907gm)
Tea, strong – ½ cup
Lemons – 3

(680gm)
Potatoes – 1 lb (454 gm)
Raisins – 1½ lbs (680gm)
Pure clover honey – 1 lb
  (454gm)
Pure white grape juice –
  3½ pints (2 litres)
or
Concentrated wine making
  white grape juice – 1 pint
  (½ litre)
Tea, strong – ½ cup
Lemons – 2

Both recipes
Yeast extract – ¼ teaspoon,
or Marmite – ¼ teaspoon, or
pure malt extract –
¼ teaspoon
and
All-purpose wine yeast
starter bottle or all-purpose
dried wine yeast or all-
purpose liquid natural wine
yeast
and
Water to 1 gallon (4½ litres)

Method – Stage 1
Put pearl barley, or flaked barley in bucket. Peel and dice potatoes. Discard peel and any green parts. Place diced potatoes in bucket. Add raisins after rinsing in warm water and chopping or mincing. Cover. Warm 1 pint (½ litre) of water in large saucepan. Stir in granulated sugar, or pure honey and yeast extract, or Marmite, or pure malt extract. When dissolved, cover and allow to cool. Then pour into bucket. For sugar-free recipe, add pure grape juice or concentrated grape juice. Cover. Both recipes – make tea, strain and allow to cool, or use strained cold tea from an

earlier brew. Discard leaves or bag. Extract juice from lemons. Discard pips, pith and peel. Place ingredients in bucket and add ¾ of wine yeast starter bottle, or the quantity directed by the supplier of the dried wine yeast, or liquid natural wine yeast. Top up to 7 pints (4 litres) with cold water. Allow at least 2″ (51mm)–4 inches (102mm) at the top of your bucket for frothing and foaming. Cover. Leave in a warm place for 10 days. Stir twice daily.

Method – Stage 2
After 10 days rack the fermenting wine from its sediment and strain into a narrow-necked 1 gallon (4½ litres) fermentation vessel. Discard solids. Top up to the neck with cold water. Cover. Leave to ferment to dryness. This can take 4–5 weeks at an even temperature of 18°C (64°F).

Wait 2 weeks after fermentation has finished; then rack wine from its sediment into a narrow-necked 1 gallon (4½ litres) storage vessel. Top up to the neck with wine of similar flavour and colour, or cold water. Fit a cork or rubber bung and keep somewhere cool for 8 months to clear and mature.

After 8 months' storage the wine should be clear and ready for bottling. Store longer if you can.

When bottled, your barley wine needs a further 2–3 months to condition before drinking.

It achieves peak perfection about 24 months after being racked into a storage vessel to clear and mature.

Beetroot

Soothing, subtle wine. Beautiful glowing colour. Ready to drink 14 months after the fermented wine has been transferred to a storage vessel to clear and mature.

Alcohol content about 15.5% alcohol per volume (27% proof).

Raisins (dried black grapes) give extra flavour, body and smoothness to this wine and nourish the wine yeast, encouraging maximum efficiency in alcohol production.

Ingredients: To make 1 gallon (4½ litres)

Country recipe
Beetroot – 4½ lbs (2Kg)
Raisins – 1 lb (454gm)
Granulated sugar – 2 lbs
    (907gm)
Tea, strong – ½ cup
Lemons – 3

Natural, sugar-free recipe
Beetroot – 4½ lbs (2Kg)
Raisins – 1½ lbs (680gm)
Pure clover honey – 1 lb
(454gm)
Pure red grape juice –
    3½ pints (2 litres)
or
Concentrated wine making
    red grape juice – 1 pint
    (½ litre)
Tea, strong – ½ cup
Lemons – 2

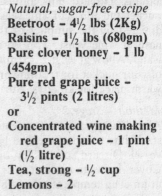

Both recipes
Yeast extract – ¼ teaspoon,
or Marmite – ¼ teaspoon, or
pure malt extract –
¼ teaspoon
and
All-purpose wine yeast
starter bottle or all-purpose
dried wine yeast or all-
purpose liquid natural wine
yeast
and
Water to 1 gallon (4½ litres)

Method – Stage 1
Cut off and discard beetroot tops and tails. Scrub and dice
beetroot (do not boil or scald) and put them in bucket. Add
raisins after rinsing in warm water and chopping or mincing.
Cover. Warm 1 pint (½ litre) of water in large saucepan. Stir
in granulated sugar, or pure honey and yeast extract, or
Marmite, or pure malt extract. When dissolved, cover and
allow to cool. Then pour into bucket. For sugar-free recipe,
add pure grape juice or concentrated grape juice. Cover.
Both recipes – make tea, strain and allow to cool, or use

strained cold tea from an earlier brew. Discard leaves or bag. Extract juice from lemons. Discard pips, pith and peel. Place ingredients in bucket and add ¾ of wine yeast starter bottle, or the quantity directed by the supplier of the dried wine yeast, or liquid natural wine yeast. Top up to 7 pints (4 litres) with cold water. Allow at least 2″ (51mm)–4 inches (102mm) at the top of your bucket for frothing and foaming. Cover. Leave in a warm place for 10 days. Stir twice daily.

Method – Stage 2
After 10 days rack the fermenting wine from its sediment and strain into a narrow-necked 1 gallon (4½ litres) fermentation vessel. Discard solids. Top up to the neck with cold water. Cover. Leave to ferment to dryness. This can take 4–5 weeks at an even temperature of 18°C (64°F).

Wait 2 weeks after fermentation has finished; then rack wine from its sediment into a narrow-necked 1 gallon (4½ litres) storage vessel. Top up to the neck with wine of similar flavour and colour, or cold water. Fit a cork or rubber bung and keep somewhere cool for 12 months to clear and mature.

After 12 months' storage the wine should be clear and ready for bottling but store up to 30 months to improve it.

When bottled, your beetroot wine needs a further 2–3 months to condition and mature before drinking.

It achieves peak perfection about 30 months after being racked into a storage vessel to clear and mature.

Blackberry

Excellent wine. Full bodied with strong flavour. Delightful colour. Ready to drink 12 months after the fermented wine has been transferred to a storage vessel to clear and mature.

Alcohol content about 13% alcohol per volume (23% proof).

Raisins (dried black grapes) give extra flavour, body and smoothness to this wine and nourish the wine yeast, encouraging maximum efficiency in alcohol production.

Ingredients: To make 1 gallon (4½ litres)

Country recipe
Blackberries – 4½ lbs (2Kg)
Raisins – 12 oz (340gm)
Granulated sugar – 2 lbs
  (907gm)
Tea, strong – ½ cup
Lemons – 2

Natural, sugar-free recipe
Blackberries – 4½ lbs (2Kg)
Raisins – 1 lb (454gm)
Pure mixed blossom honey –
  1 lb (454gm)
Pure red grape juice –
  3½ pints (2 litres)
or
**Concentrated wine making
  red grape juice** – 1 pint
  (½ litre)
Tea, strong – ½ cup
Lemon – 1

Both recipes
Yeast extract – ¼ teaspoon,
or Marmite – ¼ teaspoon, or
pure malt extract –
¼ teaspoon
and
**All-purpose wine yeast
starter bottle or all-purpose
dried wine yeast or all-
purpose liquid natural wine
yeast
and
Water to 1 gallon (4½ litres)**

Method – Stage 1
Discard fresh blackberry stalks. Lightly rinse fresh blackberries in cold water; then mash them in bucket. Add raisins
after rinsing in warm water and chopping or mincing. Cover.
Warm 1 pint (½ litre) of water in large saucepan. Stir in
granulated sugar, or pure honey and yeast extract, or
Marmite, or pure malt extract. When dissolved, cover and
allow to cool. Then pour into bucket. For sugar-free recipe,
add pure grape juice or concentrated grape juice. Cover.
Both recipes – make tea, strain and allow to cool, or use

strained cold tea from an earlier brew. Discard leaves or bag. Extract juice from lemon. Discard pips, pith and peel. Place ingredients in bucket and add ¾ of wine yeast starter bottle, or the quantity directed by the supplier of the dried wine yeast, or liquid natural wine yeast. Top up to 7 pints (4 litres) with cold water. Allow at least 2″ (51mm)–4 inches (102mm) at the top of your bucket or bin for frothing and foaming. Cover. Leave in a warm place for 10 days. Stir twice daily.

Method – Stage 2

After 10 days rack the fermenting wine from its sediment and strain into a narrow-necked 1 gallon (4½ litres) fermentation vessel. Discard solids. Top up to the neck with cold water. Cover. Leave to ferment to dryness. This can take 4–5 weeks at an even temperature of 18°C (64°F).

Wait 2 weeks after fermentation has finished; then rack wine from its sediment into a narrow-necked 1 gallon (4½ litres) storage vessel. Top up to the neck with wine of similar flavour and colour, or cold water. Fit a cork or rubber bung and keep somewhere cool for 10 months to clear and mature.

After 10 months' storage the wine should be clear and ready for bottling but a longer period should improve it.

When bottled, your blackberry wine needs a further 2–3 months to condition and mature before drinking.

It achieves peak perfection about 36 months after being racked into a storage vessel to clear and mature.

Blackcurrant

First class wine. Ready to drink 12 months after the fermented wine has been transferred to a storage vessel to clear and mature.

Alcohol content about 13% alcohol per volume (23% proof).

Raisins (dried black grapes) give extra flavour, body and smoothness to this wine and nourish the wine yeast, encouraging maximum efficiency in alcohol production.

No tea, lemons or oranges are added because black-currants are rich in natural tannin and acid.

Ingredients: To make 1 gallon (4½ litres)

Country recipe

Blackcurrants – 3¼ lbs
(1½ Kg)
Raisins – 12 oz (340gm)
Granulated sugar – 2 lbs
(907gm)

Natural, sugar-free recipe

Blackcurrants – 3¼ lbs
(1½ Kg)
Raisins – 1 lb (454gm)
Pure mixed blossom honey –
1 lb (454gm)
Pure red grape juice –
3½ pints (2 litres)
or
Concentrated wine making
red grape juice – 1 pint
(½ litre)

Both recipes

Yeast extract – ¼ teaspoon,
or Marmite – ¼ teaspoon, or
pure malt extract –
¼ teaspoon
and
All-purpose wine yeast
starter bottle or all-purpose
dried wine yeast or all-
purpose liquid natural wine
yeast
and
Water to 1 gallon (4½ litres)

Method – Stage 1

Strip fresh blackcurrants by running a fork through the stalks. Lightly rinse fresh blackcurrants in cold water; then mash them in bucket. Add raisins after rinsing in warm water and chopping or mincing. Cover. Warm 1 pint (½ litre) of water in large saucepan. Stir in granulated sugar, or pure honey and yeast extract, or Marmite, or pure malt extract. When dissolved, cover and allow to cool. Then pour into bucket. For sugar-free recipe, add pure grape juice or concentrated grape juice. Both recipes – add ¾ of wine yeast starter bottle, or the quantity directed by the supplier of the dried wine yeast, or liquid natural wine yeast. Top up to 7 pints (4 litres) with cold water. Allow at least 2″ (51mm)–4 inches (102mm) at the top of your bucket for frothing and foaming. Cover. Leave in a warm place for 10 days. Stir twice daily.

Method – Stage 2

After 10 days rack the fermenting wine from its sediment and strain into a narrow-necked 1 gallon (4½ litres) fermentation vessel. Discard solids. Top up to the neck with cold water. Cover. Leave to ferment to dryness. This can take 4–5 weeks at an even temperature of 18°C (64°F).

Wait 2 weeks after fermentation has finished; then rack wine from its sediment into a narrow-necked 1 gallon (4½ litres) storage vessel. Top up to the neck with wine of similar flavour and colour, or cold water. Fit a cork or rubber bung and keep somewhere cool for 10 months to clear and mature.

After 10 months' storage the wine should be clear and ready for bottling but a longer period can improve it.

When bottled, your blackcurrant wine needs a further 2–3 months to condition and mature before drinking.

It achieves peak perfection about 36 months after being racked into a storage vessel to clear and mature.

Carrot

Powerful and restorative tonic. An old favourite of country wine makers. Ready to drink 14 months after the fermented wine has been transferred to a storage vessel to clear and mature.

Alcohol content about 13% alcohol per volume (23% proof).

Raisins (dried black grapes) give extra flavour, body and smoothness to this wine and nourish the wine yeast, encouraging maximum efficiency in alcohol production.

Ingredients: To make 1 gallon (4½ litres)

Country recipe
Carrots – 4½ lbs (2Kg)
Potatoes – 1 lb (454gm)
Raisins – 1 lb (454gm)
Granulated sugar – 2 lbs
   (907gm)
Tea, strong – ½ cup
Lemons – 3

Natural, sugar-free recipe
Carrots – 4½ lbs (2Kg)
Potatoes – 1 lb (454gm)
Raisins – 1½ lbs (680gm)
Pure mixed blossom honey –
   1 lb (454gm)
Pure white grape juice –
   3½ pints (2 litres)
or
Concentrated wine making
   white grape juice – 1 pint
   (½ litre)
Tea, strong – ½ cup
Lemons – 2

Both recipes
Yeast extract – ¼ teaspoon,
or Marmite – ¼ teaspoon, or
pure malt extract –
¼ teaspoon
and
All-purpose wine yeast
starter bottle or all-purpose
dried wine yeast or all-
purpose liquid natural wine
yeast
and
Water to 1 gallon (4½ litres)

Method – Stage 1
Cut off and discard carrot tops and tails. Scrub and dice
carrots and put them in bucket. Peel and dice potatoes.
Discard peel and any green parts. Place diced potatoes in
bucket. Add raisins after rinsing in warm water and
chopping or mincing. Cover. Warm 1 pint (½ litre) of water
in large saucepan. Stir in granulated sugar, or pure honey

and yeast extract, or Marmite, or pure malt extract. When dissolved, cover and allow to cool. Then pour into bucket. For sugar-free recipe, add pure grape juice or concentrated grape juice. Cover. Both recipes – make tea, strain and allow to cool, or use strained cold tea from an earlier brew. Discard leaves or bag. Extract juice from lemons. Discard pips, pith and peel. Place ingredients in bucket and add ¾ of wine yeast starter bottle, or the quantity directed by the supplier of the dried wine yeast, or liquid natural wine yeast. Top up to 7 pints (4 litres) with cold water. Allow at least 2″ (51mm)–4 inches (102mm) at the top of your bucket for frothing and foaming. Cover. Leave in a warm place for 10 days. Stir twice daily.

Method – Stage 2

After 10 days rack the fermenting wine from its sediment and strain into a narrow-necked 1 gallon (4½ litres) fermentation vessel. Discard solids. Top up to the neck with cold water. Cover. Leave to ferment to dryness. This can take 4–5 weeks at an even temperature of 18°C (64°F).

Wait 2 weeks after fermentation has finished; then rack wine from its sediment into a narrow-necked 1 gallon (4½ litres) storage vessel. Top up to the neck with wine of similar flavour and colour, or cold water. Fit a cork or rubber bung and keep somewhere cool for 12 months to clear and mature.

After 12 months' storage the wine should be clear and ready for bottling, but it will go on improving up to 30 months.

When bottled, your carrot wine needs a further 2–3 months to condition and mature before drinking.

It achieves peak perfection about 30 months after being racked into a storage vessel to clear and mature.

Celery

Vital, crisp wine. Ready to drink 10 months after the fermented wine has been transferred to a storage vessel to clear and mature.

Alcohol content about 12% alcohol per volume (21% proof).

Sultanas (dried white grapes) give extra flavour, body and smoothness to this wine and nourish the wine yeast, encouraging maximum efficiency in alcohol production.

Ingredients: To make 1 gallon (4½ litres)

Country recipe
Celery stalks – 4½ lbs (2Kg)
Sultanas – 12 oz (340gm)
Granulated sugar – 2 lbs (907gm)
Tea, strong – ½ cup
Lemons – 2

Natural, sugar-free recipe
Celery stalks – 4½ lbs (2Kg)
Sultanas – 1 lb (454gm)
Pure lime blossom honey – 1 lb (454gm)
Pure white grape juice – 3½ pints (2 litres)
or
Concentrated wine making white grape juice – 1 pint (½ litre)
Tea, strong – ½ cup
Lemon – 1

Both recipes
Yeast extract – ¼ teaspoon, or Marmite – ¼ teaspoon, or pure malt extract – ¼ teaspoon
and
All-purpose wine yeast starter bottle or all-purpose dried wine yeast or all-purpose liquid natural wine yeast
and
Water to 1 gallon (4½ litres)

Method   Stage 1
To weigh fresh celery stalks, cut off and discard leaves and roots. Clean weighed fresh celery stalks in cold water; then

finely chop and put in bucket. Add sultanas after rinsing in warm water and chopping or mincing. Cover. Warm 1 pint (½ litre) of water in large saucepan. Stir in granulated sugar, or pure honey and yeast extract, or Marmite, or pure malt extract. When dissolved, cover and allow to cool. Then pour into bucket. For sugar-free recipe, add pure grape juice or concentrated grape juice. Cover. Both recipes – make tea, strain and allow to cool, or use strained cold tea from an earlier brew. Discard leaves or bag. Extract juice from lemon. Discard pips, pith and peel. Place ingredients in bucket and add ¾ of wine yeast starter bottle, or the quantity directed by the supplier of the dried wine yeast, or liquid natural wine yeast. Top up to 7 pints (4 litres) with cold water. Allow at least 2″ (51mm)–4 inches (102mm) at the top of your bucket for frothing and foaming. Cover. Leave in a warm place for 10 days. Stir twice daily.

Method – Stage 2

After 10 days rack the fermenting wine from its sediment and strain into a narrow-necked 1 gallon (4½ litres) fermentation vessel. Discard solids. Top up to the neck with cold water. Cover. Leave to ferment to dryness. This can take 4–5 weeks at an even temperature of 18°C (64°F).

Wait 2 weeks after fermentation has finished; then rack wine from its sediment into a narrow-necked 1 gallon (4½ litres) storage vessel. Top up to the neck with wine of similar flavour and colour, or cold water. Fit a cork or rubber bung and keep somewhere cool for 8 months to clear and mature.

After 8 months' storage the wine should be clear and ready for bottling but a longer period can improve it.

When bottled, your celery wine needs a further 2–3 months to condition and mature before drinking.

It achieves peak perfection about 24 months after being racked into a storage vessel to clear and mature.

Cherry

Superb wine. Glorious colour. Ready to drink 12 months after the fermented wine has been transferred to a storage vessel to clear and mature.

Alcohol content about 14% alcohol per volume (24.5% proof).

Raisins (dried black grapes) give extra flavour, body and smoothness to this wine and nourish the wine yeast, encouraging maximum efficiency in alcohol production.

Ingredients: To make 1 gallon (4½ litres)

Country recipe
Black cherries – 4½ lbs (2Kg)
Raisins – 12 oz (340gm)
Granulated sugar – 2 lbs (907gm)
Tea, strong – ½ cup
Lemons – 2

Natural, sugar-free recipe
Black cherries – 4½ lbs (2Kg)
Raisins – 1 lb (454gm)
Pure mixed blossom honey – 1 lb (454gm)
Pure red grape juice – 3½ pints (2 litres)
or
Concentrated wine making red grape juice – 1 pint (½ litre)
Tea, strong – ½ cup
Lemon – 1

Both recipes
Yeast extract – ¼ teaspoon, or Marmite – ¼ teaspoon, or pure malt extract – ¼ teaspoon
and
All-purpose wine yeast starter bottle or all-purpose dried wine yeast or all-purpose liquid natural wine yeast

and
Water to 1 gallon (4½ litres)

Method – Stage 1
Discard fresh black cherry stalks and stones. Lightly rinse
fresh cherries in cold water; then mash them in bucket. Add
raisins after rinsing in warm water and chopping or mincing.
Cover. Warm 1 pint (½ litre) of water in large saucepan. Stir
in granulated sugar, or pure honey and yeast extract, or
Marmite, or pure malt extract. When dissolved, cover and
allow to cool. Then pour into bucket. For sugar-free recipe,
add pure grape juice or concentrated grape juice. Cover.
Both recipes – make tea, strain and allow to cool, or use
strained cold tea from an earlier brew. Discard leaves or bag.
Extract juice from lemon. Discard pips, pith and peel. Place
ingredients in bucket and add ¾ of wine yeast starter bottle,
or the quantity directed by the supplier of the dried wine
yeast, or liquid natural wine yeast. Top up to 7 pints (4 litres)
with cold water. Allow at least 2″ (51mm)–4 inches (102mm)
at the top of your bucket for frothing and foaming. Cover.
Leave in a warm place for 10 days. Stir twice daily.

Method – Stage 2
After 10 days rack the fermenting wine from its sediment and
strain into a narrow-necked 1 gallon (4½ litres) fermentation
vessel. Discard solids. Top up to the neck with cold water.
Cover. Leave to ferment to dryness. This can take 4–5 weeks
at an even temperature of 18°C (64°F).

Wait 2 weeks after fermentation has finished; then rack
wine from its sediment into a narrow-necked 1 gallon (4½
litres) storage vessel. Top up to the neck with wine of similar
flavour and colour, or cold water. Fit a cork or rubber bung
and keep somewhere cool for 10 months to clear and mature.

After 10 months' storage the wine should be clear and
ready for bottling.

When bottled, your cherry wine needs a further 2–3
months to condition and mature before drinking.

It achieves peak perfection about 36 months after being
racked into a storage vessel to clear and mature if you can
manage to leave it in storage that long.

Christmas Punch

A festive drink for the season of merriment and good will.

Ingredients:

**Bottle of wine, of your
  choice – 1**
Root ginger – 2 oz (56gm)
Lemon – 1
Orange – 1
Cloves – 8
**Ground mixed spice –
  1 level teaspoon (5ml)**
**Pure honey, of your choice –
  2 heaped tablespoons**

Method

Pour wine into a large saucepan. Cover. Bruise root ginger by crushing with rolling pin or hammer. Thinly slice whole lemon and orange. Set aside some slices to float in glasses. Add all ingredients to wine in saucepan. Heat gently until warm – not boiling. Remove from heat and stir. Cover and allow to cool. Then heat again until warm; remove from heat and strain into warmed glasses. Float a small slice of lemon or orange in each glass and serve while hot.

Coltsfoot

Beautiful, succulent wine. Ready to drink 9 months after the fermented wine has been transferred to a storage vessel to clear and mature.

Alcohol content about 11.5% alcohol per volume (20% proof).

Sultanas (dried white grapes) give extra flavour, body and smoothness to this wine and nourish the wine yeast, encouraging maximum efficiency in alcohol production.

Ingredients: To make 1 gallon (4½ litres)

Country recipe

Coltsfoot heads – 2 quarts (2¼ litres)
or dried – 4 oz (113gm)
Sultanas – 8 oz (227gm)
Granulated sugar – 2 lbs (907gm)
Tea, strong – ½ cup
Oranges – 2

Natural, sugar-free recipe

Coltsfoot heads – 2 quarts (2¼ litres)
or dried – 4 oz (113gm)
Sultanas – 12 oz (340gm)
Pure orange blossom honey – 1 lb (454gm)
Pure white grape juice – 3½ pints (2 litres)
or
Concentrated wine making white grape juice – 1 pint (½ litre)
Tea, strong – ½ cup
Orange – 1

Both recipes

Yeast extract – ¼ teaspoon, or Marmite – ¼ teaspoon, or pure malt extract – ¼ teaspoon
and
All-purpose wine yeast starter bottle or all-purpose dried wine yeast or all-purpose liquid natural wine yeast
and
Water to 1 gallon (4½ litres)

Method – Stage 1

To measure fresh coltsfoot heads, discard pieces of green leaf and stalk and gently press heads in measuring jug. Lightly rinse fresh heads in cold water. Put fresh or dried heads in bucket. Add sultanas after rinsing in warm water and chopping or mincing. Cover. Warm 1 pint (½ litre) of water in large saucepan. Stir in granulated sugar, or pure honey and yeast extract, or Marmite, or pure malt extract. When dissolved, cover and allow to cool. Then pour into bucket. For sugar-free recipe, add pure grape juice or concentrated grape juice. Cover. Both recipes – make tea, strain and allow to cool, or use strained cold tea from an earlier brew. Discard leaves or bag. Extract juice from orange. Discard pips, pith and peel. Place ingredients in bucket and add ¾ of wine yeast starter bottle, or the quantity directed by the supplier of the dried wine yeast, or liquid natural wine yeast. Top up to 7 pints (4 litres) with cold water. Allow at least 2″ (51mm)–4 inches (102mm) at the top of your bucket for frothing and foaming. Cover. Leave in a warm place for 10 days. Stir twice daily.

Method – Stage 2
After 10 days rack the fermenting wine from its sediment and strain into a narrow-necked 1 gallon (4½ litres) fermentation vessel. Discard solids. Top up to the neck with cold water. Cover. Leave to ferment to dryness. This can take 4–5 weeks at an even temperature of 18°C (64°F).

Wait 2 weeks after fermentation has finished; then rack wine from its sediment into a narrow-necked 1 gallon (4½ litres) storage vessel. Top up to the neck with wine of similar flavour and colour, or cold water. Fit a cork or rubber bung and keep somewhere cool for 7 months to clear and mature.

After 7 months' storage the wine should be clear and ready for bottling. Leave it longer if you want to improve it.

When bottled, your coltsfoot wine needs a further 2–3 months to condition and mature before drinking.

It achieves peak perfection about 18 months after being racked into a storage vessel to clear and mature.

Dandelion

Splendid, golden wine. Ready to drink 9 months after the fermented wine has been transferred to a storage vessel to clear and mature.

Alcohol content about 11.5% alcohol per volume (20% proof).

Sultanas (dried white grapes) give extra flavour, body and smoothness to this wine and nourish the wine yeast, encouraging maximum efficiency in alcohol production.

Ingredients: To make 1 gallon (4½ litres)

Country recipe
**Dandelion heads – 2 quarts (2¼ litres)
or dried – 4 oz (113 gm)
Sultanas – 8 oz (227gm)
Granulated sugar – 2 lbs (907gm)
Tea, strong – ½ cup
Oranges – 2**

Natural, sugar-free recipe
**Dandelion heads – 2 quarts (2¼ litres)
or dried – 4 oz (113 gm)
Sultanas – 12 oz (340gm)
Pure orange blossom honey – 1 lb (454gm)
Pure white grape juice – 3½ pints (2 litres)
or
Concentrated wine making white grape juice – 1 pint (½ litre)
Tea, strong – ½ cup
Orange – 1**

Both recipes
**Yeast extract – ¼ teaspoon, or Marmite – ¼ teaspoon, or pure malt extract – ¼ teaspoon
and
All-purpose wine yeast starter bottle or all-purpose dried wine yeast or all-purpose liquid natural wine yeast
and
Water to 1 gallon (4½ litres)**

Method – Stage 1

To measure fresh dandelion heads, discard pieces of green leaf and stalk and gently press heads down in measuring jug. Lightly rinse fresh heads in cold water. Put fresh or dried heads in bucket. Add sultanas after rinsing in warm water and chopping or mincing. Cover. Warm 1 pint (½ litre) of water in large saucepan. Stir in granulated sugar, or pure honey and yeast extract, or Marmite, or pure malt extract. When dissolved, cover and allow to cool. Then pour into bucket. For sugar-free recipe, add pure grape juice or concentrated grape juice. Cover. Both recipes – make tea, strain and allow to cool, or use strained cold tea from an earlier brew. Discard leaves or bag. Extract juice from orange. Discard pips, pith and peel. Place ingredients in bucket and add ¾ of wine yeast starter bottle, or the quantity directed by the supplier of the dried wine yeast, or liquid natural wine yeast. Top up to 7 pints (4 litres) with cold water. Allow at least 2″ (51mm)–4 inches (102mm) at the top of your bucket for frothing and foaming. Cover. Leave in a warm place for 10 days. Stir twice daily.

Method – Stage 2

After 10 days rack the fermenting wine from its sediment and strain into a narrow-necked 1 gallon (4½ litres) fermentation vessel. Discard solids. Top up to the neck with cold water. Cover. Leave to ferment to dryness. This can take 4–5 weeks at an even temperature of 18°C (64°F).

Wait 2 weeks after fermentation has finished; then rack wine from its sediment into a narrow-necked 1 gallon (4½ litres) storage vessel. Top up to the neck with wine of similar flavour and colour, or cold water. Fit a cork or rubber bung and keep somewhere cool for 7 months to clear and mature.

After 7 months' storage the wine should be clear and ready for bottling but a longer period may improve it.

When bottled, your dandelion wine needs a further 2 3 months to condition and mature before drinking.

It achieves peak perfection about 18 months after being racked into a storage vessel to clear and mature.

Elderberry

Eminent, robust wine. Rich red colour. Ready to drink 12 months after the fermented wine has been transferred to a storage vessel to clear and mature.

Alcohol content about 13.5% alcohol per volume (24% proof).

Raisins (dried black grapes) give extra flavour, body and smoothness to this wine and nourish the wine yeast, encouraging maximum efficiency in alcohol production.

No tea is added because elderberries are rich in natural tannin.

Ingredients: To make 1 gallon (4½ litres)

Country recipe
Elderberries – 3¼ lbs
    (1½ Kg)
or dried – 12 oz (340gm)
Raisins – 12 oz (340gm)
Granulated sugar – 2 lbs
    (907gm)
Lemons – 2

Natural, sugar-free recipe
Elderberries – 3¼ lbs
    (1½ Kg)
or dried – 12 oz (340gm)
Raisins – 1 lb (454gm)
Pure mixed blossom honey –
    1 lb (454gm)
Pure red grape juice –
    3½ pints (2 litres)
or
Concentrated wine making
    red grape juice – 1 pint
    (½ litre)
Lemon – 1

Both recipes
Yeast extract – ¼ teaspoon,
or Marmite – ¼ teaspoon, or
pure malt extract –
¼ teaspoon
and
All-purpose wine yeast
starter bottle or all-purpose
dried wine yeast or all-

Elderberry—contd.

purpose liquid natural wine
yeast
and
Water to 1 gallon (4½ litres)

Method – Stage 1

Strip fresh elderberries by running a fork through the stalks.
Wear rubber gloves and an apron – the juice stains
everything it touches. Freeze the berries first, if you like, and
avoid much of the mess. Lightly rinse fresh elderberries in
cold water; then mash them in bucket. Rinse dried
elderberries in warm water; soak in cold water for 24 hours;
then mash them in bucket. Add raisins after rinsing in warm
water and chopping or mincing. Cover. Warm 1 pint (½ litre)
of water in large saucepan. Stir in granulated sugar, or pure
honey and yeast extract, or Marmite, or pure malt extract.
When dissolved, cover and allow to cool. Then pour into
bucket. For sugar-free recipe, add pure grape juice or
concentrated grape juice. Cover. Both recipes – extract juice
from lemon. Discard pips, pith and peel. Place ingredients in
bucket and add ¾ of wine yeast starter bottle, or the quantity
directed by the supplier of the dried wine yeast, or liquid
natural wine yeast. Top up to 7 pints (4 litres) with cold
water. Allow at least 2″ (51mm)–4 inches (102mm) at the top
of your bucket for frothing and foaming. Cover. Leave in a
warm place for 10 days. Stir twice daily.

Method – Stage 2

After 10 days rack the fermenting wine from its sediment and
strain into a narrow-necked 1 gallon (4½ litres) fermentation
vessel. Discard solids. Top up to the neck with cold water.
Cover. Leave to ferment to dryness. This can take 4–5 weeks
at an even temperature of 18°C (64°F).

Wait 2 weeks after fermentation has finished; then rack
wine from its sediment into a narrow-necked 1 gallon (4½
litres) storage vessel. Top up to the neck with wine of similar
flavour and colour, or cold water. Fit a cork or rubber bung
and keep somewhere cool for 10 months to clear and mature.

After 10 months' storage the wine should be clear and ready for bottling. Elderberry benefits greatly from extended storage as below.

When bottled, your elderberry wine needs a further 2–3 months to condition and mature before drinking.

It achieves peak perfection about 42 months after being racked into a storage vessel to clear and mature.

Elderflower

Supremely fragrant, light wine. Ready to drink 8 months after the fermented wine has been transferred to a storage vessel to clear and mature.

*Elderflowers make a particularly pleasant sparkling wine, see page 83.

Alcohol content about 10% alcohol per volume (17.5% proof).

Sultanas (dried white grapes) give extra flavour, body and smoothness to this wine and nourish the wine yeast, encouraging maximum efficiency in alcohol production.

Ingredients: To make 1 gallon (4½ litres)

Country recipe
**Elderflowers – 1 pint
  (½ litre)
or dried – 1 oz (28gm)
Sultanas – 8 oz (227gm)
Granulated sugar – 1¾ lbs
  (794gm)
Tea, strong – ½ cup
Lemons – 2**

Natural, sugar-free recipe
**Elderflowers – 1 pint
  (½ litre)
or dried – 1 oz (28gm)
Sultanas – 12 oz (340gm)
Pure lime blossom honey –
  12 oz (340gm)
Pure white grape juice –
  3½ pints (2 litres)
or
Concentrated wine making
  white grape juice – 1 pint
  (½ litre)
Tea, strong – ½ cup
Lemon – 1**

Elderflower—contd.

Both recipes
**Yeast extract – ¼ teaspoon,
or Marmite – ¼ teaspoon, or
pure malt extract –
¼ teaspoon
and
All-purpose wine yeast
starter bottle or all-purpose
dried wine yeast or all-
purpose liquid natural wine
yeast
and
Water to 1 gallon (4½ litres)**

Method – Stage 1

To measure fresh elderflowers, discard pieces of green leaf
and stem and gently press flowers in measuring jug. Lightly
rinse fresh flowers in cold water. Put fresh or dried flowers in
bucket. Add sultanas after rinsing in warm water and
chopping or mincing. Cover. Warm 1 pint (½ litre) of water
in large saucepan. Stir in granulated sugar, or pure honey
and yeast extract, or Marmite, or pure malt extract. When
dissolved, cover and allow to cool. Then pour into bucket.
For sugar-free recipe, add pure grape juice or concentrated
grape juice. Cover. Both recipes – make tea, strain and allow
to cool, or use strained cold tea from an earlier brew.
Discard leaves or bag. Extract juice from lemon. Discard
pips, pith and peel. Place ingredients in bucket and add ¾ of
wine yeast starter bottle, or the quantity directed by the
supplier of the dried wine yeast, or liquid natural wine yeast.
Top up to 7 pints (4 litres) with cold water. Allow at least 2″
(51mm) 4 inches (102mm) at the top of your bucket for
frothing and foaming. Cover. Leave in a warm place for 10
days. Stir twice daily.

Method   Stage 2

After 10 days rack the fermenting wine from its sediment and
strain into a narrow-necked 1 gallon (4½ litres) fermentation

vessel. Discard solids. Top up to the neck with cold water. Cover. Leave to ferment to dryness. This can take 4–5 weeks at an even temperature of 18°C (64°F).

Wait 2 weeks after fermentation has finished; then rack wine from its sediment into a narrow-necked 1 gallon (4½ litres) storage vessel. Top up to the neck with wine of similar flavour and colour, or cold water. Do NOT add potassium sorbate (see page 47) to your wine if you intend to make it sparkle. Fit a cork or rubber bung and keep somewhere cool for 6 months to clear and mature.

After 6 months' storage the wine should be clear and ready for bottling.

When bottled, your elderflower wine needs a further 2–3 months to condition and mature before drinking.

It achieves peak perfection about 18 months after being racked into a storage vessel to clear and mature if you can bear to leave it in storage that long.

Ginger

Strong, warming wine. Ready to drink 10 months after the fermented wine has been transferred to a storage vessel to clear and mature.

Alcohol content about 13% alcohol per volume (23% proof).

Sultanas (dried white grapes) give extra flavour, body and smoothness to this wine and nourish the wine yeast, encouraging maximum efficiency in alcohol production.

Ingredients: To make 1 gallon (4½ litres)

Country recipe	*Natural, sugar-free recipe*
Root ginger – 6 oz (170gm)	**Root ginger – 6 oz (170gm)**
Sultanas – 1 lb (454gm)	**Sultanas – 1½ lb (680gm)**
Granulated sugar – 2 lbs (907gm)	**Pure lime blossom honey – 1 lb (454gm)**
Tea, strong – ½ cup	**Pure white grape juice –**

Ginger—contd.

Oranges – 5

3½ pints (2 litres)
or
Concentrated wine making white grape juice – 1 pint (½ litre)
Tea, strong – ½ cup
Oranges – 4

Both recipes
Yeast extract – ¼ teaspoon, or Marmite – ¼ teaspoon, or pure malt extract – ¼ teaspoon
and
All-purpose wine yeast starter bottle or all-purpose dried wine yeast or all-purpose liquid natural wine yeast
and
Water to 1 gallon (4½ litres)

Method – Stage 1

Bruise root ginger by crushing with rolling pin or hammer. Put bruised ginger in bucket. Add sultanas after rinsing in warm water and chopping or mincing. Cover. Warm 1 pint (½ litre) of water in large saucepan. Stir in granulated sugar, or pure honey and yeast extract, or Marmite, or pure malt extract. When dissolved, cover and allow to cool. Then pour into bucket. For sugar-free recipe, add pure grape juice or concentrated grape juice. Cover. Both recipes – make tea, strain and allow to cool, or use strained cold tea from an earlier brew. Discard leaves or bag. Extract juice from oranges. Discard pips, pith and peel. Place ingredients in bucket and add ¾ of wine yeast starter bottle, or the quantity directed by the supplier of the dried wine yeast, or liquid natural wine yeast. Top up to 7 pints (4 litres) with cold water. Allow at least 2″ (51mm)–4 inches (102mm) at the top

of your bucket for frothing and foaming. Cover. Leave in a
warm place for 10 days. Stir twice daily.

Method – Stage 2
After 10 days rack the fermenting wine from its sediment and
strain into a narrow-necked 1 gallon (4½ litres) fermentation
vessel. Discard solids. Top up to the neck with cold water.
Cover. Leave to ferment to dryness. This can take 4–5 weeks
at an even temperature of 18°C (64°F).

Wait 2 weeks after fermentation has finished; then rack
wine from its sediment into a narrow-necked 1 gallon (4½
litres) storage vessel. Top up to the neck with wine of similar
flavour and colour, or cold water. Fit a cork or rubber bung
and keep somewhere cool for 8 months to clear and mature.

After 8 months' storage the wine should be clear and ready
for bottling but a longer spell in storage can improve it.

When bottled, your ginger wine needs a further 2–3
months to condition and mature before drinking.

It achieves peak perfection about 24 months after being
racked into a storage vessel to clear and mature.

Gooseberry

Light, fruity and refreshing table wine. Ready to drink 11
months after the fermented wine has been transferred to a
storage vessel to clear and mature.
*Gooseberries make a particularly pleasant sparkling wine,
see page 83.

Alcohol content about 11% alcohol per volume (19%
proof).

Sultanas (dried white grapes) give extra flavour, body and
smoothness to this wine and nourish the wine yeast,
encouraging maximum efficiency in alcohol production.

Ingredients: To make 1 gallon (4½ litres)

Country recipe	*Natural, sugar-free recipe*
Gooseberries – 3¼ lbs	**Gooseberries – 3¼ lbs**
(1½ Kg)	**(1½ Kg)**

Gooseberry—contd.

Sultanas - 12 oz (340gm)
Granulated sugar - 1¾ lbs
  (794gm)
Tea, strong - ½ cup
Oranges - 2

Sultanas - 1 lb (454gm)
Pure acacia blossom honey -
  12 oz (340gm)
Pure white grape juice -
  3½ pints (2 litres)
or
Concentrated wine making
  white grape juice - 1 pint
  (½ litre)
Tea, strong - ½ cup
Orange - 1

Both recipes
Yeast extract - ¼ teaspoon,
or Marmite - ¼ teaspoon, or
pure malt extract -
¼ teaspoon
and
All-purpose wine yeast
starter bottle or all-purpose
dried wine yeast or all-
purpose liquid natural wine
yeast
and
Water to 1 gallon (4½ litres)

Method   Stage 1
Discard gooseberry tops and tails. Lightly rinse gooseberries in cold water; then mash them in bucket. Add sultanas after rinsing in warm water and chopping or mincing. Cover. Warm 1 pint (½ litre) of water in large saucepan. Stir in granulated sugar, or pure honey and yeast extract, or Marmite, or pure malt extract. When dissolved, cover and allow to cool. Then pour into bucket. For sugar-free recipe, add pure grape juice or concentrated grape juice. Cover. Both recipes – make tea, strain and allow to cool, or use strained cold tea from an earlier brew. Discard leaves or bag. Extract juice from orange. Discard pips, pith and peel. Place

ingredients in bucket and add ¾ of wine yeast starter bottle, or the quantity directed by the supplier of the dried wine yeast, or liquid natural wine yeast. Top up to 7 pints (4 litres) with cold water. Allow at least 2″ (51mm)–4 inches (102mm) at the top of your bucket for frothing and foaming. Cover. Leave in a warm place for 10 days. Stir twice daily.

Method – Stage 2

After 10 days rack the fermenting wine from its sediment and strain into a narrow-necked 1 gallon (4½ litres) fermentation vessel. Discard solids. Top up to the neck with cold water. Cover. Leave to ferment to dryness. This can take 4–5 weeks at an even temperature of 18°C (64°F).

Wait 2 weeks after fermentation has finished; then rack wine from its sediment into a narrow-necked 1 gallon (4½ litres) storage vessel. Top up to the neck with wine of similar flavour and colour, or cold water. Do NOT add potassium sorbate (see page 47) to your wine if you intend to make it sparkle. Fit a cork or rubber bung and keep somewhere cool for 9 months to clear and mature.

After 9 months' storage the wine should be clear and ready for bottling. Store it longer if you can.

When bottled, your gooseberry wine needs a further 2–3 months to condition and mature before drinking.

It achieves peak perfection about 24 months after being racked into a storage vessel to clear and mature.

Hawthorn Blossom

Delicate, velvet smooth wine. Ready to drink 8 months after the fermented wine has been transferred to a storage vessel to clear and mature.

Alcohol content about 11.5% alcohol per volume (20% proof).

Sultanas (dried white grapes) give extra flavour, body and smoothness to this wine and nourish the wine yeast, encouraging maximum efficiency in alcohol production.

Ingredients: To make 1 gallon (4½ litres)

Country recipe
Hawthorn blossom –
  2 quarts (2¼ litres)
Sultanas – 8 oz (227gm)
Granulated sugar – 2 lbs
  (907gm)
Tea, strong – ½ cup
Oranges – 2

Natural, sugar-free recipe
Hawthorn blossom –
  2 quarts (2¼ litres)
Sultanas – 12 oz (340gm)
Pure orange blossom honey
  – 1 lb (454gm)
Pure white grape juice –
  3½ pints (2 litres)
or
Concentrated wine making
  white grape juice – 1 pint
  (½ litre)
Tea, strong – ½ cup
Orange – 1

Both recipes
Yeast extract – ¼ teaspoon,
or Marmite – ¼ teaspoon, or
pure malt extract –
¼ teaspoon
and
All-purpose wine yeast
starter bottle or all-purpose
dried wine yeast or all-
purpose liquid natural wine
yeast
and
Water to 1 gallon (4½ litres)

Method - Stage 1
To measure fresh hawthorn blossom, discard pieces of green leaf and stem and gently press blossom in measuring jug. Lightly rinse fresh blossom in cold water. Put blossom in bucket. Add sultanas after rinsing in warm water and chopping or mincing. Cover. Warm 1 pint (½ litre) of water in large saucepan. Stir in granulated sugar, or pure honey and yeast extract, or Marmite, or pure malt extract. When dissolved, cover and allow to cool. Then pour into bucket.

For sugar-free recipe, add pure grape juice or concentrated grape juice. Cover. Both recipes – make tea, strain and allow to cool, or use strained cold tea from an earlier brew. Discard leaves or bag. Extract juice from orange. Discard pips, pith and peel. Place ingredients in bucket and add ¾ of wine yeast starter bottle, or the quantity directed by the supplier of the dried wine yeast, or liquid natural wine yeast. Top up to 7 pints (4 litres) with cold water. Allow at least 2″ (51mm)–4 inches (102mm) at the top of your bucket for frothing and foaming. Cover. Leave in a warm place for 10 days. Stir twice daily.

Method – Stage 2
After 10 days rack the fermenting wine from its sediment and strain into a narrow-necked 1 gallon (4½ litres) fermentation vessel. Discard solids. Top up to the neck with cold water. Cover. Leave to ferment to dryness. This can take 4–5 weeks at an even temperature of 18°C (64°F).

Wait 2 weeks after fermentation has finished; then rack wine from its sediment into a narrow-necked 1 gallon (4½ litres) storage vessel. Top up to the neck with wine of similar flavour and colour, or cold water. Fit a cork or rubber bung and keep somewhere cool for 6 months to clear and mature.

After 6 months' storage the wine should be clear and ready for bottling but a longer period can improve it.

When bottled, your hawthorn blossom wine needs a further 2–3 months to condition and mature before drinking.

It achieves peak perfection about 18 months after being racked into a storage vessel to clear and mature.

Hop

Calming, flavourful wine. Gather hop cones from female flowers in July/August, or use dried hops. Ready to drink 10 months after the fermented wine has been transferred to a storage vessel to clear and mature.

Alcohol content about 11.5% alcohol per volume (20% proof).

Sultanas (dried white grapes) give extra flavour, body and smoothness to this wine and nourish the wine yeast, encouraging maximum efficiency in alcohol production.

Ingredients: To make 1 gallon (4½ litres)

Country recipe

Hop cones – 2 quarts (2¼ litres)
or dried – 4 oz (113gm)
Sultanas – 8 oz (227gm)
Granulated sugar – 2 lbs (907gm)
Tea, strong – ½ cup
Lemons – 2

Natural, sugar-free recipe

Hop cones – 2 quarts (2¼ litres)
or dried – 4 oz (113gm)
Sultanas – 12 oz (340gm)
Pure clover honey – 1 lb (454gm)
Pure white grape juice – 3½ pints (2 litres)
or
Concentrated wine making white grape juice – 1 pint (½ litre)
Tea, strong – ½ cup
Lemon – 1

Both recipes

Yeast extract – ¼ teaspoon, or Marmite – ¼ teaspoon, or pure malt extract – ¼ teaspoon
and
All-purpose wine yeast starter bottle or all-purpose dried wine yeast or all-purpose liquid natural wine yeast
and
Water to 1 gallon (4½ litres)

Method – Stage 1

To measure fresh hop cones, discard pieces of green leaf and stalk and gently press cones in measuring jug. Lightly rinse fresh cones in cold water. Put fresh or dried hops in bucket. Add sultanas after rinsing in warm water and chopping or mincing. Cover. Warm 1 pint (½ litre) of water in large saucepan. Stir in granulated sugar, or pure honey and yeast extract, or Marmite, or pure malt extract. When dissolved, cover and allow to cool. Then pour into bucket. For sugar-free recipe, add pure grape juice or concentrated grape juice. Cover. Both recipes – make tea, strain and allow to cool, or use strained cold tea from an earlier brew. Discard leaves or bag. Extract juice from lemon. Discard pips, pith and peel. Place ingredients in bucket and add ¾ of wine yeast starter bottle, or the quantity directed by the supplier of the dried wine yeast, or liquid natural wine yeast. Top up to 7 pints (4 litres) with cold water. Allow at least 2″ (51mm)–4 inches (102mm) at the top of your bucket for frothing and foaming. Cover. Leave in a warm place for 10 days. Stir twice daily.

Method – Stage 2
After 10 days rack the fermenting wine from its sediment and strain into a narrow-necked 1 gallon (4½ litres) fermentation vessel. Discard solids. Top up to the neck with cold water. Cover. Leave to ferment to dryness. This can take 4–5 weeks at an even temperature of 18°C (64°F).

Wait 2 weeks after fermentation has finished; then rack wine from its sediment into a narrow-necked 1 gallon (4½ litres) storage vessel. Top up to the neck with wine of similar flavour and colour, or cold water. Fit a cork or rubber bung and keep somewhere cool for 8 months to clear and mature.

After 8 months' storage the wine should be clear and ready for bottling. Store longer if you can.

When bottled, your hop wine needs a further 2–3 months to condition and mature before drinking.

It achieves peak perfection about 18 months after being racked into a storage vessel to clear and mature.

Mead

Richly distinctive beverage. Different types of pure honey produce different styles of mead. Ready to drink 12 months after the fermented mead has been transferred to a storage vessel to clear and mature.

Alcohol content about 17% alcohol per volume (30% proof).

Sultanas (dried white grapes) give extra flavour, body and smoothness to mead and nourish the wine yeast, encouraging maximum efficiency in alcohol production.

Ingredients:

Country, sugar-free recipe
Pure honey, of your choice –
  3¼ lbs (1½ Kg)
Sultanas – 12 oz (340gm)
Tea, strong – ½ cup
Lemons – 2
Yeast extract – ¼ teaspoon,
or Marmite – ¼ teaspoon, or
pure malt extract –
¼ teaspoon
All-purpose wine yeast
starter bottle or all-purpose
dried wine yeast or all-
purpose liquid natural wine
yeast
Water to 1 gallon (4½ litres)

Method – Stage 1

Warm 1¾ pints (1 litre) of water in large saucepan. Stir in pure honey and yeast extract, or Marmite, or pure malt extract. When dissolved, cover and allow to cool. Rinse sultanas in warm water and chop or mince. Make tea, strain and allow to cool, or use strained cold tea from an earlier brew. Discard leaves or bag. Extract juice from lemons. Discard pips, pith and peel. Place ingredients in bucket and add ¾ of wine yeast starter bottle, or the quantity directed by the supplier of the dried wine yeast, or liquid natural wine yeast. Top up to 7 pints (4 litres) with cold water. Allow at least 2" (51mm)–4 inches (102mm) at the top of your bucket for frothing and foaming. Cover. Leave in a warm place for 10 days. Stir twice daily.

Method – Stage 2

After 10 days rack the fermenting mead from its sediment and strain into a narrow-necked 1 gallon (4½ litres) fermentation vessel. Discard solids. Top up to the neck with cold water. Cover. Leave to ferment to dryness. This can take 4–5 weeks at an even temperature of 18°C (64°F).

Wait 2 weeks after fermentation has finished; then rack mead from its sediment into a narrow-necked 1 gallon (4½ litres) storage vessel. Top up to the neck with mead or wine of similar colour, or cold water. Fit a cork or rubber bung and keep somewhere cool for 10 months to clear and mature.

After 10 months' storage the mead should be clear and ready for bottling.

When bottled, your mead needs a further 2–3 months to condition and mature before drinking.

It achieves peak perfection about 36 months after being racked into a storage vessel to clear and mature if you can manage to leave it in storage that long.

Nettle

Most palatable wine. Young nettles are best. Ready to drink 9 months after the fermented wine has been transferred to a storage vessel to clear and mature.

Alcohol content about 12% alcohol per volume (21% proof).

Sultanas (dried white grapes) give extra flavour, body and smoothness to this wine and nourish the wine yeast, encouraging maximum efficiency in alcohol production.

Ingredients: To make 1 gallon (4½ litres)

Country recipe

Nettle tops – 2 quarts
  (2¼ litres)
Sultanas – 12 oz (340gm)
Granulated sugar – 2 lbs
  (907gm)
Tea, strong – ½ cup
Lemons – 2

Natural, sugar-free recipe

Nettle tops – 2 quarts
  (2 ¼ litres)
Sultanas – 1 lb (454gm)
Pure clover honey – 1 lb
  454gm)
Pure white grape juice –
  3½ pints (2 litres)
or
**Concentrated wine making
  white grape juice** – 1 pint
  (½ litre)
Tea, strong – ½ cup
Lemon – 1

Both recipes

Yeast extract – ¼ teaspoon,
or Marmite – ¼ teaspoon, or
pure malt extract –
¼ **teaspoon**
and
**All-purpose wine yeast
starter bottle or all-purpose
dried wine yeast or all-
purpose liquid natural wine
yeast**
and
Water to 1 gallon (4½ litres)

Method – Stage 1

To measure fresh nettle tops, cut off and discard stalks and gently press tops in measuring jug. Lightly rinse fresh tops in cold water. Put tops in bucket. Add sultanas after rinsing in warm water and chopping or mincing. Cover. Warm 1 pint (½ litre) of water in large saucepan. Stir in granulated sugar, or pure honey and yeast extract, or Marmite, or pure malt extract. When dissolved, cover and allow to cool. Then pour into bucket. For sugar-free recipe, add pure grape juice or concentrated grape juice. Cover. Both recipes – make tea, strain and allow to cool, or use strained cold tea from an earlier brew. Discard leaves or bag. Extract juice from lemon. Discard pips, pith and peel. Place ingredients in bucket and add ¾ of wine yeast starter bottle, or the quantity directed by the supplier of the dried wine yeast, or liquid natural wine yeast. Top up to 7 pints (4 litres) with cold water. Allow at least 2″ (51mm)–4 inches (102mm) at the top of your bucket for frothing and foaming. Cover. Leave in a warm place for 10 days. Stir twice daily.

Method – Stage 2
After 10 days rack the fermenting wine from its sediment and strain into a narrow-necked 1 gallon (4½ litres) fermentation vessel. Discard solids. Top up to the neck with cold water. Cover. Leave to ferment to dryness. This can take 4–5 weeks at an even temperature of 18°C (64°F).

Wait 2 weeks after fermentation has finished; then rack wine from its sediment into a narrow-necked 1 gallon (4½ litres) storage vessel. Top up to the neck with wine of similar flavour and colour, or cold water. Fit a cork or rubber bung and keep somewhere cool for 7 months to clear and mature.

After 7 months' storage the wine should be clear and ready for bottling.

When bottled, your nettle wine needs a further 2–3 months to condition and mature before drinking.

It achieves peak perfection about 20 months after being racked into a storage vessel to clear and mature if you can bear to have it in storage for that bit longer.

Oak Leaf

Pleasing wine, with lots of bite. Ready to drink 10 months after the fermented wine has been transferred to a storage vessel to clear and mature.

Alcohol content about 11.5% alcohol per volume (20% proof).

Sultanas (dried white grapes) give extra flavour, body and smoothness to this wine and nourish the wine yeast, encouraging maximum efficiency in alcohol production.

No tea is added because oak leaves are rich in natural tannin.

Ingredients: To make 1 gallon (4½ litres)

Country recipe
Oak leaves – 1 gallon (4½ litres)
Sultanas – 8 oz (227gm)
Granulated sugar – 2 lbs (907gm)
Lemons – 2

Natural, sugar-free recipe
Oak leaves – 1 gallon (4½ litres)
Sultanas – 12 oz (340gm)
Pure clover honey – 1 lb (454gm)
Pure white grape juice – 3½ pints (2 litres)
or
Concentrated wine making white grape juice – 1 pint (½ litre)
Lemon – 1

Both recipes
Yeast extract – ¼ teaspoon, or Marmite – ¼ teaspoon, or pure malt extract – ¼ teaspoon
and
All-purpose wine yeast starter bottle or all-purpose dried wine yeast or all-purpose liquid natural wine yeast
and
Water to 1 gallon (4½ litres)

Method – Stage 1
To measure fresh oak leaves, cut off and discard stalks and gently press leaves in measuring jug or calibrated bucket. Lightly rinse fresh leaves in cold water. Put leaves in bucket.

Add sultanas after rinsing in warm water and chopping or mincing. Cover. Warm 1 pint (½ litre) of water in large saucepan. Stir in granulated sugar, or pure honey and yeast extract, or Marmite, or pure malt extract. When dissolved, cover and allow to cool. Then pour into bucket. For sugar-free recipe, add pure grape juice or concentrated grape juice. Cover. Both recipes – extract juice from lemon. Discard pips, pith and peel. Place ingredients in bucket and add ¾ of wine yeast starter bottle, or the quantity directed by the supplier of the dried wine yeast, or liquid natural wine yeast. Top up to 7 pints (4 litres) with cold water. Allow at least 2″ (51mm)–4 inches (102mm) at the top of your bucket for frothing and foaming. Cover. Leave in a warm place for 10 days. Stir twice daily.

Method – Stage 2
After 10 days rack the fermenting wine from its sediment and strain into a narrow-necked 1 gallon (4½ litres) fermentation vessel. Discard solids. Top up to the neck with cold water. Cover. Leave to ferment to dryness. This can take 4–5 weeks at an even temperature of 18°C (64°F).

Wait 2 weeks after fermentation has finished; then rack wine from its sediment into a narrow-necked 1 gallon (4½ litres) storage vessel. Top up to the neck with wine of similar flavour and colour, or cold water. Fit a cork or rubber bung and keep somewhere cool for 8 months to clear and mature.

After 8 months' storage the wine should be clear and ready for bottling. Store it for longer to improve it, if you wish.

When bottled, your oak leaf wine needs a further 2–3 months to condition and mature before drinking.

It achieves peak perfection about 20 months after being racked into a storage vessel to clear and mature.

Parsley

Agreeable and flavourful wine. Ready to drink 10 months after the fermented wine has been transferred to a storage vessel to clear and mature.

Alcohol content about 11.5% alcohol per volume (20% proof).

Sultanas (dried white grapes) give extra flavour, body and smoothness to this wine and nourish the wine yeast, encouraging maximum efficiency in alcohol production.

Ingredients: To make 1 gallon (4½ litres)

Country recipe
**Parsley heads – 1 lb (454gm)
or dried – 4 oz (113 gm)
Sultanas – 8 oz (227gm)
Granulated sugar – 2 lbs
   (907gm)
Tea, strong – ½ cup
Lemons – 2**

Natural, sugar-free recipe
**Parsley heads – 1 lb (454gm)
or dried – 4 oz (113 gm)
Sultanas – 12 oz (340gm)
Pure acacia blossom honey –
   1 lb (454gm)
Pure white grape juice –
   3½ pints (2 litres)
or
Concentrated wine making
   white grape juice – 1 pint
   (½ litre)
Tea, strong – ½ cup
Lemon – 1**

Both recipes
**Yeast extract – ¼ teaspoon,
or Marmite – ¼ teaspoon, or
pure malt extract –
¼ teaspoon
and
All-purpose wine yeast
starter bottle or all-purpose
dried wine yeast or all-
purpose liquid natural wine
yeast
and
Water to 1 gallon (4½ litres)**

Method – Stage 1

To weigh fresh parsley heads, cut off and discard stems. Lightly rinse weighed fresh heads in cold water. Put fresh or dried heads in bucket. Add sultanas after rinsing in warm water and chopping or mincing. Cover. Warm 1 pint (½ litre) of water in large saucepan. Stir in granulated sugar, or pure honey and yeast extract, or Marmite, or pure malt extract. When dissolved, cover and allow to cool. Then pour into bucket. For sugar-free recipe, add pure grape juice or concentrated grape juice. Cover. Both recipes – make tea, strain and allow to cool, or use strained cold tea from an earlier brew. Discard leaves or bag. Extract juice from lemon. Discard pips, pith and peel. Place ingredients in bucket and add ¾ of wine yeast starter bottle, or the quantity directed by the supplier of the dried wine yeast, or liquid natural wine yeast. Top up to 7 pints (4 litres) with cold water. Allow at least 2″ (51mm)–4 inches (102mm) at the top of your bucket for frothing and foaming. Cover. Leave in a warm place for 10 days. Stir twice daily.

Method – Stage 2

After 10 days rack the fermenting wine from its sediment and strain into a narrow-necked 1 gallon (4½ litres) fermentation vessel. Discard solids. Top up to the neck with cold water. Cover. Leave to ferment to dryness. This can take 4–5 weeks at an even temperature of 18°C (64°F).

Wait 2 weeks after fermentation has finished; then rack wine from its sediment into a narrow-necked 1 gallon (4½ litres) storage vessel. Top up to the neck with wine of similar flavour and colour, or cold water. Fit a cork or rubber bung and keep somewhere cool for 8 months to clear and mature.

After 8 months' storage the wine should be clear and ready for bottling but a longer spell of storage can improve it.

When bottled, your parsley wine needs a further 2–3 months to condition and mature before drinking.

It achieves peak perfection about 20 months after being racked into a storage vessel to clear and mature.

Parsnip

Good wine. Ready to drink 16 months after after the fermented wine has been transferred to a storage vessel to clear and mature.

Alcohol content about 13% alcohol per volume (23% proof).

Sultanas (dried white grapes) give extra flavour, body and smoothness to this wine and nourish the wine yeast, encouraging maximum efficiency in alcohol production.

Ingredients: To make 1 gallon (4½ litres)

Country recipe
Parsnips – 4½ lbs (2Kg)
Potatoes – 1 lb (454gm)
Sultanas – 1 lb (454gm)
Granulated sugar – 2 lbs (907gm)
Tea, strong – ½ cup
Lemons – 3

Natural, sugar-free recipe
Parsnips – 4½ lbs (2Kg)
Potatoes – 1 lb (454gm)
Sultanas – 1½ lbs (680gm)
Pure clover honey – 1 lb (454gm)
Pure white grape juice – 3½ pints (2 litres)
or
Concentrated wine making white grape juice – 1 pint (½ litre)
Tea, strong – ½ cup
Lemons – 2

Both recipes
Yeast extract – ¼ teaspoon, or Marmite – ¼ teaspoon, or pure malt extract – ¼ teaspoon
and
All-purpose wine yeast starter bottle or all-purpose dried wine yeast or all-purpose liquid natural wine yeast
and
Water to 1 gallon (4½ litres)

Method – Stage 1

Cut off and discard parsnip tops and tails. Scrub and dice parsnips and put them in bucket. Peel and dice potatoes. Discard peel and any green parts. Place diced potatoes in bucket. Add sultanas after rinsing in warm water and chopping or mincing. Cover. Warm 1 pint (½ litre) of water in large saucepan. Stir in granulated sugar, or pure honey and yeast extract, or Marmite, or pure malt extract. When dissolved, cover and allow to cool. Then pour into bucket. For sugar-free recipe, add pure grape juice or concentrated grape juice. Cover. Both recipes – make tea, strain and allow to cool, or use strained cold tea from an earlier brew. Discard leaves or bag. Extract juice from lemons. Discard pips, pith and peel. Place ingredients in bucket and add ¾ of wine yeast starter bottle, or the quantity directed by the supplier of the dried wine yeast, or liquid natural wine yeast. Top up to 7 pints (4 litres) with cold water. Allow at least 2″ (51mm)–4 inches (102mm) at the top of your bucket for frothing and foaming. Cover. Leave in a warm place for 10 days. Stir twice daily.

Method – Stage 2

After 10 days rack the fermenting wine from its sediment and strain into a narrow-necked 1 gallon (4½ litres) fermentation vessel. Discard solids. Top up to the neck with cold water. Cover. Leave to ferment to dryness. This can take 4–5 weeks at an even temperature of 18°C (64°F).

Wait 2 weeks after fermentation has finished; then rack wine from its sediment into a narrow-necked 1 gallon (4½ litres) storage vessel. Top up to the neck with wine of similar flavour and colour, or cold water. Fit a cork or rubber bung and keep somewhere cool for 14 months to clear and mature.

After 14 months' storage the wine should be clear and ready for bottling. Store it longer if you can.

When bottled, your parsnip wine needs a further 2–3 months to condition and mature before drinking.

It achieves peak perfection about 36 months after being racked into a storage vessel to clear and mature.

Peach

Luscious wine. Attractive colour. Ready to drink 10 months after the fermented wine has been transferred to a storage vessel to clear and mature.

*Peaches make a particularly pleasant sparkling wine, see page 83.

Alcohol content about 11.5% alcohol per volume (20% proof).

Sultanas (dried white grapes) give extra flavour, body and smoothness to this wine and nourish the wine yeast, encouraging maximum efficiency in alcohol production.

Ingredients: To make 1 gallon (4½ litres)

Country recipe
Peaches – 3¼ lbs (1½Kg)
or dried – 10 oz (283gm)
Sultanas – 12 oz (340gm)
Granulated sugar – 1¾ lbs
  (794gm)
Tea, strong – ½ cup
Oranges – 2

Natural, sugar-free recipe
Peaches – 3¼ lbs (1½Kg)
or dried – 10 oz (283gm)
Sultanas – 1 lb (454gm)
Pure orange blossom honey
  – 12 oz (340gm)
Pure white grape juice –
  3½ pints (2 litres)
or
Concentrated wine making
  white grape juice – 1 pint
  (½ litre)
Tea, strong – ½ cup
Orange – 1

Both recipes
Yeast extract – ¼ teaspoon,
or Marmite – ¼ teaspoon, or
pure malt extract –
¼ teaspoon
and
All-purpose wine yeast
starter bottle or all-purpose
dried wine yeast or all-

**purpose liquid natural wine
yeast
and
Water to 1 gallon (4½ litres)**

Method – Stage 1

Cut fresh peaches in half and discard stones. Lightly rinse
fresh peaches in cold water; then mash them in bucket. Rinse
dried peaches in warm water; chop or mince and put in
bucket. Add sultanas after rinsing in warm water and
chopping or mincing. Cover. Warm 1 pint (½ litre) of water
in large saucepan. Stir in granulated sugar, or pure honey
and yeast extract, or Marmite, or pure malt extract. When
dissolved, cover and allow to cool. Then pour into bucket.
For sugar-free recipe, add pure grape juice or concentrated
grape juice. Cover. Both recipes – make tea, strain and allow
to cool, or use strained cold tea from an earlier brew.
Discard leaves or bag. Extract juice from orange. Discard
pips, pith and peel. Place ingredients in bucket and add ¾ of
wine yeast starter bottle, or the quantity directed by the
supplier of the dried wine yeast, or liquid natural wine yeast.
Top up to 7 pints (4 litres) with cold water. Allow at least 2"
(51mm)–4 inches (102mm) at the top of your bucket for
frothing and foaming. Cover. Leave in a warm place for 10
days. Stir twice daily.

Method – Stage 2

After 10 days rack the fermenting wine from its sediment and
strain into a narrow-necked 1 gallon (4½ litres) fermentation
vessel. Discard solids. Top up to the neck with cold water.
Cover. Leave to ferment to dryness. This can take 4–5 weeks
at an even temperature of 18°C (64°F).

Wait 2 weeks after fermentation has finished; then rack
wine from its sediment into a narrow-necked 1 gallon (4½
litres) storage vessel. Top up to the neck with wine of similar
flavour and colour, or cold water. Do NOT add potassium
sorbate (see page 47) to your wine if you intend to make it
sparkle. Fit a cork or rubber bung and keep somewhere cool
for 8 months to clear and mature.

After 8 months' storage the wine should be clear and ready

for bottling

When bottled, your peach wine needs a further 2–3 months to condition and mature before drinking.

It achieves peak perfection about 24 months after being racked into a storage vessel to clear and mature if you can manage to leave it in storage that long.

Peppermint

Refreshing tonic. Ready to drink 9 months after the fermented wine has been transferred to a storage vessel to clear and mature.

Alcohol content about 11.5% alcohol per volume (20% proof).

Sultanas (dried white grapes) give extra flavour, body and smoothness to this wine and nourish the wine yeast, encouraging maximum efficiency in alcohol production.

Ingredients: To make 1 gallon (4½ litres)

Country recipe
Peppermint leaves –
   1¾ pints (1 litre)
or dried – 2 oz (56gm)
Sultanas – 8 oz (227gm)
Granulated sugar – 2 lbs
   (907gm)
Tea, strong – ½ cup
Lemons – 2

Natural, sugar-free recipe
Peppermint leaves –
   1¾ pints (1 litre)
or dried – 2 oz (56gm)
Sultanas – 12 oz (340gm)
Pure lime blossom honey –
   1 lb (454gm)
Pure white grape juice –
   3½ pints (2 litres)
or
Concentrated wine making
   white grape juice – 1 pint
   (½ litre)
Tea, strong – ½ cup
Lemon – 1

Both recipes
Yeast extract – ¼ **teaspoon,
or Marmite –** ¼ **teaspoon, or
pure malt extract –**
¼ **teaspoon
and
All-purpose wine yeast
starter bottle or all-purpose
dried wine yeast or all-
purpose liquid natural wine
yeast
and
Water to 1 gallon (4**½ **litres)**

Method – Stage 1
To measure fresh peppermint leaves, discard pieces of stalk
and gently press leaves in measuring jug. Lightly rinse fresh
leaves in cold water. Put fresh or dried leaves in bucket. Add
sultanas after rinsing in warm water and chopping or
mincing. Cover. Warm 1 pint (½ litre) of water in large
saucepan. Stir in granulated sugar, or pure honey and yeast
extract, or Marmite, or pure malt extract. When dissolved,
cover and allow to cool. Then pour into bucket. For sugar-
free recipe, add pure grape juice or concentrated grape juice.
Cover. Both recipes – make tea, strain and allow to cool, or
use strained cold tea from an earlier brew. Discard leaves or
bag. Extract juice from lemon. Discard pips, pith and peel.
Place ingredients in bucket and add ¾ of wine yeast starter
bottle, or the quantity directed by the supplier of the dried
wine yeast, or liquid natural wine yeast. Top up to 7 pints (4
litres) with cold water. Allow at least 2″ (51mm)–4 inches
(102mm) at the top of your bucket for frothing and foaming.
Cover. Leave in a warm place for 10 days. Stir twice daily.

Method – Stage 2
After 10 days rack the fermenting wine from its sediment and
strain into a narrow-necked 1 gallon (4½ litres) fermentation
vessel. Discard solids. Top up to the neck with cold water.
Cover. Leave to ferment to dryness. This can take 4–5 weeks
at an even temperature of 18°C (64°F).

Wait 2 weeks after fermentation has finished; then rack wine from its sediment into a narrow-necked 1 gallon (4½ litres) storage vessel. Top up to the neck with wine of similar flavour and colour, or cold water. Fit a cork or rubber bung and keep somewhere cool for 7 months to clear and mature.

After 7 months' storage the wine should be clear and ready for bottling but a longer period should improve it.

When bottled, your peppermint wine needs a further 2–3 months to condition and mature before drinking.

It achieves peak perfection about 18 months after being racked into a storage vessel to clear and mature.

Plum

Lovely wine. Beautiful colour. Ready to drink 12 months after the fermented wine has been transferred to a storage vessel to clear and mature.

Alcohol content about 13.5% alcohol per volume (24% proof).

Sultanas (dried white grapes) give extra flavour, body and smoothness to this wine and nourish the wine yeast, encouraging maximum efficiency in alcohol production.

Ingredients: To make 1 gallon (4½ litres)

Country recipe	Natural, sugar-free recipe
Plums – 4½ lbs (2Kg)	Plums – 4½ lbs (2Kg)
or dried (prunes) – 1 lb (454gm)	or dried (prunes) – 1 lb (454gm)
Sultanas – 12 oz (340gm)	Sultanas – 1 lb (454gm)
Granulated sugar – 2 lbs (907gm)	Pure mixed blossom honey – 1 lb (454gm)
Tea, strong – ½ cup	Pure white grape juice – 3½ pints (2 litres)
Oranges – 2	or
	Concentrated wine making white grape juice – 1 pint (½ litre)

Tea, strong – ½ cup
Orange – 1

Both recipes
**Yeast extract – ¼ teaspoon,
or Marmite – ¼ teaspoon, or
pure malt extract –
¼ teaspoon
and
All-purpose wine yeast
starter bottle or all-purpose
dried wine yeast or all-
purpose liquid natural wine
yeast
and
Water to 1 gallon (4½ litres)**

Method – Stage 1
Remove and discard fresh plum stones. Lightly rinse fresh
plums in cold water; then mash them in bucket. Rinse dried
plums (prunes) in warm water; soak them in cold water for
24 hours; then remove and discard stones and mash prunes
in bucket. Add sultanas after rinsing in warm water and
chopping or mincing. Cover. Warm 1 pint (½ litre) of water
in large saucepan. Stir in granulated sugar, or pure honey
and yeast extract, or Marmite, or pure malt extract. When
dissolved, cover and allow to cool. Then pour into bucket.
For sugar-free recipe, add pure grape juice or concentrated
grape juice. Cover. Both recipes – make tea, strain and allow
to cool, or use strained cold tea from an earlier brew.
Discard leaves or bag. Extract juice from orange. Discard
pips, pith and peel. Place ingredients in bucket and add ¾ of
wine yeast starter bottle, or the quantity directed by the
supplier of the dried wine yeast, or liquid natural wine yeast.
Top up to 7 pints (4 litres) with cold water. Allow at least 2″
(51mm)–4 inches (102mm) at the top of your bucket for
frothing and foaming. Cover. Leave in a warm place for 10
days. Stir twice daily.

Method – Stage 2
After 10 days rack the fermenting wine from its sediment and

strain into a narrow-necked 1 gallon (4½ litres) fermentation vessel. Discard solids. Top up to the neck with cold water. Cover. Leave to ferment to dryness. This can take 4–5 weeks at an even temperature of 18°C (64°F).

Wait 2 weeks after fermentation has finished; then rack wine from its sediment into a narrow-necked 1 gallon (4½ litres) storage vessel. Top up to the neck with wine of similar flavour and colour, or cold water. Fit a cork or rubber bung and keep somewhere cool for 10 months to clear and mature.

After 10 months' storage the wine should be clear and ready for bottling but a longer period can improve it.

When bottled, your plum wine needs a further 2–3 months to condition and mature before drinking.

It achieves peak perfection about 24 months after being racked into a storage vessel to clear and mature.

Raspberry

Radiant rosé wine. Ready to drink 12 months after the fermented wine has been transferred to a storage vessel to clear and mature.

Alcohol content about 12.5% alcohol per volume (22% proof).

Sultanas (dried white grapes) give extra flavour, body and smoothness to this wine and nourish the wine yeast, encouraging maximum efficiency in alcohol production.

Ingredients: To make 1 gallon (4½ litres)

Country recipe	*Natural, sugar-free recipe*
Raspberries – 3¼ lbs (1½ Kg)	Raspberries – 3¼ lbs (1½ Kg)
Sultanas – 12 oz (340gm)	Sultanas – 1 lb (454gm)
Granulated sugar – 2 lbs (907gm)	Pure orange blossom honey – 1 lb (454gm)
Tea, strong – ½ cup	Pure white grape juice – 3½ pints (2 litres)
Oranges – 2	or
	Concentrated wine making

white grape juice – 1 pint
(½ litre)
Tea, strong – ½ cup
Orange – 1

Both recipes
**Yeast extract – ¼ teaspoon,
or Marmite – ¼ teaspoon, or
pure malt extract –
¼ teaspoon
and
All-purpose wine yeast
starter bottle or all-purpose
dried wine yeast or all-
purpose liquid natural wine
yeast
and
Water to 1 gallon (4½ litres)**

Method – Stage 1
Remove and discard pieces of green leaf and stalk from fresh
raspberries. Lightly rinse fresh raspberries in cold water;
then mash them in bucket. Add sultanas after rinsing in
warm water and chopping or mincing. Cover. Warm 1 pint
(½ litre) of water in large saucepan. Stir in granulated sugar,
or pure honey and yeast extract, or Marmite, or pure malt
extract. When dissolved, cover and allow to cool. Then pour
into bucket. For sugar-free recipe, add pure grape juice or
concentrated grape juice. Cover. Both recipes – make tea,
strain and allow to cool, or use strained cold tea from an
earlier brew. Discard leaves or bag. Extract juice from
orange. Discard pips, pith and peel. Place ingredients in
bucket and add ¾ of wine yeast starter bottle, or the quantity
directed by the supplier of the dried wine yeast, or liquid
natural wine yeast. Top up to 7 pints (4 litres) with cold
water. Allow at least 2″ (51mm)–4 inches (102mm) at the top
of your bucket for frothing and foaming. Cover. Leave in a
warm place for 10 days. Stir twice daily.

Method – Stage 2
After 10 days rack the fermenting wine from its sediment and

strain into a narrow-necked 1 gallon (4½ litres) fermentation vessel. Discard solids. Top up to the neck with cold water. Cover. Leave to ferment to dryness. This can take 4–5 weeks at an even temperature of 18°C (64°F).

Wait 2 weeks after fermentation has finished; then rack wine from its sediment into a narrow-necked 1 gallon (4½ litres) storage vessel. Top up to the neck with wine of similar flavour and colour, or cold water. Fit a cork or rubber bung and keep somewhere cool for 10 months to clear and mature.

After 10 months' storage the wine should be clear and ready for bottling. Store longer if you can.

When bottled, your raspberry wine needs a further 2–3 months to condition and mature before drinking.

It achieves peak perfection about 30 months after being racked into a storage vessel to clear and mature.

Rice and Raisin

Bright, revitalizing wine. Ready to drink 8 months after the fermented wine has been transferred to a storage vessel to clear and mature.

Alcohol content about 13% alcohol per volume (23% proof).

Raisins (dried black grapes) give extra flavour, body and smoothness to this wine and nourish the wine yeast, encouraging maximum efficiency in alcohol production.

Ingredients: To make 1 gallon (4½ litres)

Country recipe	*Natural, sugar-free recipe*
Brown rice – 1 lb (454gm)	Brown rice – 1 lb (454gm)
Raisins – 1 lb (454gm)	Raisins – 1½ lbs (680gm)
Granulated sugar – 2 lbs (907gm)	Pure acacia blossom honey – 1 lb (454gm)
Tea, strong – ½ cup	Pure red grape juice –
Lemons – 3	3½ pints (2 litres)
	or

**Concentrated wine making
red grape juice – 1 pint
(½ litre)
Tea, strong – ½ cup
Lemons – 2**

Both recipes
**Yeast extract – ¼ teaspoon,
or Marmite – ¼ teaspoon, or
pure malt extract –
¼ teaspoon
and
All-purpose wine yeast
starter bottle or all-purpose
dried wine yeast or all-
purpose liquid natural wine
yeast
and
Water to 1 gallon (4½ litres)**

Method   Stage 1
Put brown rice in bucket. Add raisins after rinsing in warm
water and chopping or mincing. Cover. Warm 1 pint (½ litre)
of water in large saucepan. Stir in granulated sugar, or pure
honey and yeast extract, or Marmite, or pure malt extract.
When dissolved, cover and allow to cool. Then pour into
bucket. For sugar-free recipe, add pure grape juice or
concentrated grape juice. Cover. Both recipes make tea,
strain and allow to cool, or use strained cold tea from an
earlier brew. Discard leaves or bag. Extract juice from
lemons. Discard pips, pith and peel. Place ingredients in
bucket and add ¾ of wine yeast starter bottle, or the quantity
directed by the supplier of the dried wine yeast, or liquid
natural wine yeast. Top up to 7 pints (4 litres) with cold
water. Allow at least 2″ (51mm) 4 inches (102mm) at the top
of your bucket for frothing and foaming. Cover. Leave in a
warm place for 10 days. Stir twice daily.

Method   Stage 2
After 10 days rack the fermenting wine from its sediment and

strain into a narrow-necked 1 gallon (4½ litres) fermentation vessel. Discard solids. Top up to the neck with cold water. Cover. Leave to ferment to dryness. This can take 4–5 weeks at an even temperature of 18°C (64°F).

Wait 2 weeks after fermentation has finished; then rack wine from its sediment into a narrow-necked 1 gallon (4½ litres) storage vessel. Top up to the neck with wine of similar flavour and colour, or cold water. Fit a cork or rubber bung and keep somewhere cool for 6 months to clear and mature.

After 6 months' storage the wine should be clear and ready for bottling. Store for longer to improve it, if you can.

When bottled, your rice and raisin wine needs a further 2–3 months to condition and mature before drinking.

It achieves peak perfection about 24 months after being racked into a storage vessel to clear and mature.

Rose Petal

Smooth, appetizing, fragrant wine. You can mix colours and varieties. Ready to drink 8 months after the fermented wine has been transferred to a storage vessel to clear and mature.

*Rose petals make a particularly pleasant sparkling wine, see page 83.

Alcohol content about 10% alcohol per volume (17.5% proof).

Sultanas (dried white grapes) give extra flavour, body and smoothness to this wine and nourish the wine yeast, encouraging maximum efficiency in alcohol production.

Ingredients: To make 1 gallon (4½ litres)

Country recipe	*Natural, sugar-free recipe*
Rose petals – 2 quarts (2¼ litres)	**Rose petals – 2 quarts (2¼ litres)**
or dried – 4 oz (113gm)	**or dried – 4 oz (113gm)**
Sultanas – 8 oz (227gm)	**Sultanas – 12 oz (340gm)**

Granulated sugar – 1¾ lbs
(794gm)
Tea, strong – ½ cup
Oranges – 2

Pure orange blossom honey
– 12 oz (340gm)
Pure white grape juice –
3½ pints (2 litres)

or

Concentrated wine making
white grape juice – 1 pint
(½ litre)
Tea, strong – ½ cup
Orange – 1

Both recipes
Yeast extract – ¼ teaspoon,
or Marmite – ¼ teaspoon, or
pure malt extract –
¼ teaspoon
and
All-purpose wine yeast
starter bottle or all-purpose
dried wine yeast or all-
purpose liquid natural wine
yeast
and
Water to 1 gallon (4½ litres)

Method – Stage 1
To measure fresh rose petals, gently press petals in
measuring jug. Lightly rinse fresh petals in cold water. Put
fresh or dried petals in bucket. Add sultanas after rinsing in
warm water and chopping or mincing. Cover. Warm 1 pint
(½ litre) of water in large saucepan. Stir in granulated sugar,
or pure honey and yeast extract, or Marmite, or pure malt
extract. When dissolved, cover and allow to cool. Then pour
into bucket. For sugar-free recipe, add pure grape juice or
concentrated grape juice. Cover. Both recipes – make tea,
strain and allow to cool, or use strained cold tea from an
earlier brew. Discard leaves or bag. Extract juice from
orange. Discard pips, pith and peel. Place ingredients in
bucket and add ¾ of wine yeast starter bottle, or the quantity
directed by the supplier of the dried wine yeast, or liquid

natural wine yeast. Top up to 7 pints (4 litres) with cold water. Allow at least 2″(51mm)–4 inches (102mm) at the top of your bucket for frothing and foaming. Cover. Leave in a warm place for 10 days. Stir twice daily.

Method – Stage 2

After 10 days rack the fermenting wine from its sediment and strain into a narrow-necked 1 gallon (4½ litres) fermentation vessel. Discard solids. Top up to the neck with cold water. Cover. Leave to ferment to dryness. This can take 4–5 weeks at an even temperature of 18°C (64°F).

Wait 2 weeks after fermentation has finished; then rack wine from its sediment into a narrow-necked 1 gallon (4½ litres) storage vessel. Top up to the neck with wine of similar flavour and colour, or cold water. Do NOT add potassium sorbate (see page 47) to your wine if you intend to make it sparkle. Fit a cork or rubber bung and keep somewhere cool for 6 months to clear and mature.

After 6 months' storage the wine should be clear and ready for bottling but a longer period is likely to improve it.

When bottled, your rose petal wine needs a further 2–3 months to condition and mature before drinking.

It achieves peak perfection about 18 months after being racked into a storage vessel to clear and mature.

Rosehip

Cheering, silky wine. Ready to drink 10 months after the fermented wine has been transferred to a storage vessel to clear and mature.

Alcohol content about 12% alcohol per volume (21% proof).

Raisins (dried black grapes) give extra flavour, body and smoothness to this wine and nourish the wine yeast, encouraging maximum efficiency in alcohol production.

Ingredients: To make 1 gallon (4½ litres)

Country recipe
**Rosehips – 2¼ lbs (1Kg)
or dried – 8 oz (227gm)
Raisins – 12 oz (340gm)
Granulated sugar – 2 lbs
    (907gm)
Tea, strong – ½ cup
Oranges – 2**

Natural, sugar-free recipe
**Rosehips – 2¼ lbs (1Kg)
or dried – 8 oz (227gm)
Raisins – 1 lb (454gm)
Pure lime blossom honey –
    1 lb (454gm)
Pure red grape juice –
    3½ pints (2 litres)
or
Concentrated wine making
    red grape juice – 1 pint
    (½ litre)
Tea, strong – ½ cup
Orange – 1**

Both recipes
**Yeast extract – ¼ teaspoon,
or Marmite – ¼ teaspoon, or
pure malt extract –
¼ teaspoon
and
All-purpose wine yeast
starter bottle or all-purpose
dried wine yeast or all-
purpose liquid natural wine
yeast
and
Water to 1 gallon (4½ litres)**

Method   Stage 1
Remove and discard pieces of stalk from fresh rosehips.
Lightly rinse fresh rosehips in cold water; then mash them in
bucket. Rinse dried rosehips in warm water; soak in cold
water for 24 hours; then mash them in bucket. Add raisins
after rinsing in warm water and chopping or mincing. Cover.
Warm 1 pint (½ litre) of water in large saucepan. Stir in
granulated sugar, or pure honey and yeast extract, or
Marmite, or pure malt extract. When dissolved, cover and
allow to cool. Then pour into bucket. For sugar-free recipe,
add pure grape juice or concentrated grape juice. Cover.

Both recipes - make tea, strain and allow to cool, or use strained cold tea from an earlier brew. Discard leaves or bag. Extract juice from orange. Discard pips, pith and peel. Place ingredients in bucket and add ¾ of wine yeast starter bottle, or the quantity directed by the supplier of the dried wine yeast, or liquid natural wine yeast. Top up to 7 pints (4 litres) with cold water. Allow at least 2″ (51mm)–4 inches (102mm) at the top of your bucket for frothing and foaming. Cover. Leave in a warm place for 10 days. Stir twice daily.

Method – Stage 2

After 10 days rack the fermenting wine from its sediment and strain into a narrow-necked 1 gallon (4½ litres) fermentation vessel. Discard solids. Top up to the neck with cold water. Cover. Leave to ferment to dryness. This can take 4–5 weeks at an even temperature of 18°C (64°F).

Wait 2 weeks after fermentation has finished; then rack wine from its sediment into a narrow-necked 1 gallon (4½ litres) storage vessel. Top up to the neck with wine of similar flavour and colour, or cold water. Fit a cork or rubber bung and keep somewhere cool for 8 months to clear and mature.

After 8 months' storage the wine should be clear and ready for bottling. Store longer if you can.

When bottled, your rosehip wine needs a further 2-3 months to condition and mature before drinking.

It achieves peak perfection about 20 months after being racked into a storage vessel to clear and mature.

Sloe

Noble, medium bodied table wine. Ready to drink 12 months after the fermented wine has been transferred to a storage vessel to clear and mature.

Alcohol content about 12.5% alcohol per volume (22% proof).

Raisins (dried black grapes) give extra flavour, body and smoothness to this wine and nourish the wine yeast, encouraging maximum efficiency in alcohol production.

Ingredients: To make 1 gallon (4½ litres)

Country recipe
Sloes – 2 lbs (907gm)
or dried – 11 oz (312gm)
Raisins – 12 oz (340gm)
Granulated sugar – 2 lbs
   (907gm)
Tea, strong – ½ cup
Oranges – 2

Natural, sugar-free recipe
Sloes – 2 lbs (907gm)
or dried – 11 oz (312gm)
Raisins – 1 lb (454gm)
Pure mixed blossom honey –
   1 lb (454gm)
Pure red grape juice –
   3½ pints (2 litres)
or
Concentrated wine making
   red grape juice – 1 pint
   (½ litre)
Tea, strong – ½ cup
Orange – 1

Both recipes
Yeast extract – ¼ teaspoon,
or Marmite – ¼ teaspoon, or
pure malt extract –
¼ teaspoon
and
All-purpose wine yeast
starter bottle or all-purpose
dried wine yeast or all-
purpose liquid natural wine
yeast
and
Water to 1 gallon (4½ litres)

Method   Stage 1
Remove and discard fresh sloe stalks. The small stone in the
fruit is difficult to remove and best left. Lightly rinse fresh
sloes in cold water; then mash them in bucket. Rinse dried
sloes in warm water; soak in cold water for 24 hours; then
mash them in bucket. Add raisins after rinsing in warm
water and chopping or mincing. Cover. Warm 1 pint (½ litre)
of water in large saucepan. Stir in granulated sugar, or pure
honey and yeast extract, or Marmite, or pure malt extract.
When dissolved, cover and allow to cool. Then pour into

bucket. For sugar-free recipe, add pure grape juice or concentrated grape juice. Cover. Both recipes make tea, strain and allow to cool, or use strained cold tea from an earlier brew. Discard leaves or bag. Extract juice from orange. Discard pips, pith and peel. Place ingredients in bucket and add ¾ of wine yeast starter bottle, or the quantity directed by the supplier of the dried wine yeast, or liquid natural wine yeast. Top up to 7 pints (4 litres) with cold water. Allow at least 2″ (51mm)–4 inches (102mm) at the top of your bucket for frothing and foaming. Cover. Leave in a warm place for 10 days. Stir twice daily.

Method   Stage 2
After 10 days rack the fermenting wine from its sediment and strain into a narrow-necked 1 gallon (4½ litres) fermentation vessel. Discard solids. Top up to the neck with cold water. Cover. Leave to ferment to dryness. This can take 4 5 weeks at an even temperature of 18°C (64°F).

Wait 2 weeks after fermentation has finished; then rack wine from its sediment into a narrow-necked 1 gallon (4½ litres) storage vessel. Top up to the neck with wine of similar flavour and colour, or cold water. Fit a cork or rubber bung and keep somewhere cool for 10 months to clear and mature.

After 10 months' storage the wine should be clear and ready for bottling.

When bottled, your sloe wine needs a further 2 3 months to condition and mature before drinking.

It achieves peak perfection about 36 months after being racked into a storage vessel to clear and mature. It is worth being patient and storing as long as you can up to the 3 years.

Strawberry

Tantalizing light wine. Ready to drink 12 months after the fermented wine has been transferred to a storage vessel to clear and mature.

*Strawberries make a particularly pleasant sparkling wine, see page 83.

Alcohol content about 11.5% alcohol per volume (20% proof).

Sultanas (dried white grapes) give extra flavour, body and smoothness to this wine and nourish the wine yeast, encouraging maximum efficiency in alcohol production.

Ingredients: To make 1 gallon (4½ litres)

Country recipe
Strawberries – 3¼ (1½Kg)
Sultanas – 12 oz (340gm)
Granulated sugar – 1¾ lbs (794gm)
Tea, strong – ½ cup
Oranges – 2

Natural, sugar-free recipe
Strawberries – 3¼ lbs (1½Kg)
Sultanas – 1 lb (454gm)
Pure orange blossom honey – 12 oz (340gm)
Pure white grape juice – 3½ pints (2 litres)
or
Concentrated wine making white grape juice – 1 pint (½ litre)
Tea, strong – ½ cup
Orange – 1

Both recipes
Yeast extract – ¼ teaspoon, or Marmite – ¼ teaspoon, or pure malt extract – ¼ teaspoon
and
All-purpose wine yeast starter bottle or all-purpose dried wine yeast or all-purpose liquid natural wine yeast
and
Water to 1 gallon (4½ litres)

Method   Stage 1
Remove and discard pieces of green leaf and stalk from fresh strawberries. Lightly rinse fresh strawberries in cold water;

then mash them in bucket. Add sultanas after rinsing in warm water and chopping or mincing. Cover. Warm 1 pint (½ litre) of water in large saucepan. Stir in granulated sugar, or pure honey and yeast extract, or Marmite, or pure malt extract. When dissolved, cover and allow to cool. Then pour into bucket. For sugar-free recipe, add pure grape juice or concentrated grape juice. Cover. Both recipes – make tea, strain and allow to cool, or use strained cold tea from an earlier brew. Discard leaves or bag. Extract juice from orange. Discard pips, pith and peel. Place ingredients in bucket and add ¾ of wine yeast starter bottle, or the quantity directed by the supplier of the dried wine yeast, or liquid natural wine yeast. Top up to 7 pints (4 litres) with cold water. Allow at least 2″ (51mm)–4 inches (102mm) at the top of your bucket for frothing and foaming. Cover. Leave in a warm place for 10 days. Stir twice daily.

Method – Stage 2

After 10 days rack the fermenting wine from its sediment and strain into a narrow-necked 1 gallon (4½ litres) fermentation vessel. Discard solids. Top up to the neck with cold water. Cover. Leave to ferment to dryness. This can take 4–5 weeks at an even temperature of 18°C (64°F).

Wait 2 weeks after fermentation has finished; then rack wine from its sediment into a narrow-necked 1 gallon (4½ litres) storage vessel. Top up to the neck with wine of similar flavour and colour, or cold water. Do NOT add potassium sorbate (see page 47) to your wine if you intend to make it sparkle. Fit a cork or rubber bung and keep somewhere cool for 10 months to clear and mature.

After 10 months' storage the wine should be clear and ready for bottling.

When bottled, your strawberry wine needs a further 2–3 months to condition and mature before drinking.

It achieves peak perfection about 24 months after being racked into a storage vessel to clear and mature if you can manage to leave it in storage that long.

Tea And Prune

Invigorating, full bodied wine. For a lighter tea wine, use extra sultanas instead of prunes. Ready to drink 11 months after the fermented wine has been transferred to a storage vessel to clear and mature.

Alcohol content about 13.5% alcohol per volume (24% proof).

Sultanas (dried white grapes) give extra flavour, body and smoothness to this wine and nourish the wine yeast, encouraging maximum efficiency in alcohol production.

Ingredients: To make 1 gallon (4½ litres)

Country recipe
Tea, strong – 3 cups
Prunes (dried) – 12 oz (340gm)
Sultanas – 12 oz (340gm)
Granulated sugar – 2 lbs (907gm)
Lemons – 3

Natural, sugar-free recipe
Tea, strong – 3 cups
Prunes (dried) – 12 oz (340gm)
Sultanas – 1 lb (454gm)
Pure clover honey – 1 lb (454gm)
Pure white grape juice – 3½ pints (2 litres)
or
Concentrated wine making white grape juice – 1 pint (½ litre)
Lemons – 2

Both recipes
Yeast extract – ¼ teaspoon, or Marmite – ¼ teaspoon, or pure malt extract – ¼ teaspoon
and
All-purpose wine yeast starter bottle or all-purpose dried wine yeast or all-purpose liquid natural wine yeast

Tea And Prune—contd.

and Water to 1 gallon (4½ litres)

Method – Stage 1

Rinse prunes in warm water; soak them in cold water for 24 hours; then remove and discard stones and mash prunes in bucket. Add sultanas after rinsing in warm water and chopping or mincing. Cover. Warm 1 pint (½ litre) of water in large saucepan. Stir in granulated sugar, or pure honey and yeast extract, or Marmite, or pure malt extract. When dissolved, cover and allow to cool. Then pour into bucket. For sugar-free recipe, add pure grape juice or concentrated grape juice. Cover. Both recipes – make tea, strain and allow to cool, or use strained cold tea from an earlier brew. Discard leaves or bags. Extract juice from lemons. Discard pips, pith and peel. Place ingredients in bucket and add ¾ of wine yeast starter bottle, or the quantity directed by the supplier of the dried wine yeast, or liquid natural wine yeast. Top up to 7 pints (4 litres) with cold water. Allow at least 2″ (51mm)–4 inches (102mm) at the top of your bucket for frothing and foaming. Cover. Leave in a warm place for 10 days. Stir twice daily.

Method – Stage 2

After 10 days rack the fermenting wine from its sediment and strain into a narrow-necked 1 gallon (4½ litres) fermentation vessel. Discard solids. Top up to the neck with cold water. Cover. Leave to ferment to dryness. This can take 4–5 weeks at an even temperature of 18°C (64°F).

Wait 2 weeks after fermentation has finished; then rack wine from its sediment into a narrow-necked 1 gallon (4½ litres) storage vessel. Top up to the neck with wine of similar flavour and colour, or cold water. Fit a cork or rubber bung and keep somewhere cool for 9 months to clear and mature.

After 9 months' storage the wine should be clear and ready for bottling but a longer period can improve it.

When bottled, your tea and prune wine needs a further 2–3 months to condition and mature before drinking.

It achieves peak perfection about 24 months after being racked into a storage vessel to clear and mature.